VOLUNTEERS IN PUBLIC SCHOOLS

Bernard Michael, Editor

Committee on the Use of Volunteers in Schools

Commission on Behavioral and
Social Sciences and Education

National Research Council

NATIONAL ACADEMY PRESS
Washington, D.C. 1990

NATIONAL ACADEMY PRESS • 2101 Constitution Avenue, NW • Washington, DC 20418

NOTICE: The project that is the subject of this report was approved by the Governing Board of the National Research Council, whose members are drawn from the councils of the National Academy of Sciences, the National Academy of Engineering, and the Institute of Medicine. The members of the committee responsible for the report were chosen for their special competences and with regard for appropriate balance.

This report has been reviewed by a group other than the authors according to procedures approved by a Report Review Committee consisting of members of the National Academy of Sciences, the National Academy of Engineering, and the Institute of Medicine.

The National Academy of Sciences is a private, nonprofit, self-perpetuating society of distinguished scholars engaged in scientific and engineering research, dedicated to the furtherance of science and technology and to their use for the general welfare. Upon the authority of the charter granted to it by the Congress in 1863, the Academy has a mandate that requires it to advise the federal government on scientific and technical matters. Dr. Frank Press is president of the National Academy of Sciences.

The National Academy of Engineering was established in 1964, under the charter of the National Academy of Sciences, as a parallel organization of outstanding engineers. It is autonomous in its administration and in the selection of its members, sharing with the National Academy of Sciences the responsibility for advising the federal government. The National Academy of Engineering also sponsors engineering programs aimed at meeting national needs, encourages education and research, and recognizes the superior achievements of engineers. Dr. Robert M. White is president of the National Academy of Engineering.

The Institute of Medicine was established in 1970 by the National Academy of Sciences to secure the services of eminent members of appropriate professions in the examination of policy matters pertaining to the health of the public. The Institute acts under the responsibility given to the National Academy of Sciences by its congressional charter to be an adviser to the federal government and, upon its own initiative, to identify issues of medical care, research, and education. Dr. Samuel O. Thier is president of the Institute of Medicine.

The National Research Council was organized by the National Academy of Sciences in 1916 to associate the broad community of science and technology with the Academy's purposes of furthering knowledge and advising the federal government. Functioning in accordance with general policies determined by the Academy, the Council has become the principal operating agency of both the National Academy of Sciences and the National Academy of Engineering in providing services to the government, the public, and the scientific and engineering communities. The Council is administered jointly by both Academies and the Institute of Medicine. Dr. Frank Press and Dr. Robert M. White are chairman and vice chairman, respectively, of the National Research Council.

The work that provided the basis for this volume was supported by the U.S. Department of Education under contract LC 88061001.

Library of Congress Cataloging-in-Publication Data
National Research Council (U.S.). Committee on the Use of Volunteers
    in Schools.
        Volunteers in public schools / Bernard Michael, editor; Committee
    on the Use of Volunteers in Schools, Commission on Behavioral and
    Social Sciences and Education, National Research Council.
            p.   cm.
        Includes bibliographical references (p.).
        ISBN 0-309-04149-X
        1. Volunteer workers in education--United States. I. Michael,
    Bernard. II. Title.
    LB2844.1.V6N36 1990
    371.2'02--dc20   89-49273
                                                              CIP

Committee on the Use of Volunteers in Schools

LEONARD BICKMAN *(Chair)*, Department of Psychology and Human Development, Vanderbilt University

JOHN W. ALDEN, Alden Marketing Group, Inc., Alexandria, Va.

STEPHEN DIAZ, School of Education, California State University, San Bernardino

PAUL L. EVANS, IBM Educational Systems, Atlanta, Ga.

MARVIN LAZERSON, Graduate School of Education, University of Pennsylvania

FLORETTA DUKES MCKENZIE, The McKenzie Group, Washington, D.C.

DANIEL MERENDA, National School Volunteer Program, Inc., Alexandria, Va.

CAROL MOCK, Department of Political Science, University of Illinois

PENELOPE PETERSON, Institute for Research on Teaching, Michigan State University

JOYCE ROGERS, Portland, Maine

GILBERT SEWALL, Teachers College, Columbia University

MANYA UNGAR, The National PTA, Chicago, Ill.

CAROL WEISS, Graduate School of Education, Harvard University

BARBARA J. YENTZER, National Education Association, Washington, D.C.

BERNARD MICHAEL, Study Director
DANIEL LEVINE, Consultant
VIRGINIA ROBINSON, Consultant
EVELYN SIMEON, Administrative Secretary
CAROLE ANN FOOTE, Administrative Secretary

Acknowledgments

The committee wishes to thank the many people who contributed to the preparation of this report. First, I want to express appreciation to my colleagues on the committee for their generous contributions of time and expert knowledge. Many of them prepared materials that were included in the report, and virtually all members contributed to the various drafts. Our report and especially the recommendations are a synthesis of their efforts, ideas, and insights on the issues addressed.

The mandate for this study was the result of legislation introduced by Senator Daniel J. Evans of Washington; Lisa Marchese, his legislative counsel, provided valuable insights to the committee and staff.

Alan Ginsburg, director of the U.S. Department of Education's Office of Planning and Evaluation Service, which funded the project, participated in the committee's early discussions, helping to provide background for the study; Arthur Kirschenbaum, the study's project monitor, provided helpful advice and assistance to the committee throughout the conduct of this study, and his efforts are deeply appreciated.

Staff of the National Center for Education Statistics (NCES) were extremely helpful in making available preliminary tabulations from the NCES School and Staffing Survey for use in this report. We are particularly indebted to Emerson Elliott, director of the center, and Mary Papageorgiou and Charles Hammer, who generously provided unpublished data.

Special thanks are also due the directors and staffs of volunteer programs at the 13 sites visited by committee members, particularly the key people who organized the visits and patiently answered our questions: Carol Tice, Ann Arbor, Michigan; Betsy Nelson, Boston, Massachusetts; Frances Holliday, Chicago, Illinois; Maureen Hopkins, Contra Costa

County, California; Sue Guinn, Corsicana, Texas; Carol Renick and Linda Brown, Dade County, Florida; Rosemary Morice and Sharlene Block, Dallas, Texas; Sally Jackson, Montgomery County, Maryland; Sandy Schniepp, Kingfield, Maine; Heidi McGinley, Augusta, Maine; Sandra Treacy, San Francisco, California; Artis Slipsager, Studio City, California; Nancy McDonald, Tulsa, Oklahoma; and Connie Spinner, Washington, D.C.

We also thank the many school superintendents, principals, teachers, volunteers, and students who helped us to gain a better understanding of what makes school volunteer programs successful.

Ramsey Sheldon of the Council of Chief State School Officers was most helpful in assisting and advising the staff on gathering information from states on their volunteer activities. Similarly, Jane Asche, Virginia Cooperative Extension Services, contributed her time and efforts in reviewing the annotated bibliography.

Of course, major thanks are due the Committee on the Use of Volunteers in Schools, consisting of distinguished individuals appointed by the chairman of the National Research Council (NRC). Members represent the relevant scientific disciplines (for example, evaluation research, sociology, political science, education); the practitioner community (school administration, teaching, volunteer programs); and other fields such as business. Members of NRC committees are volunteers themselves. They receive no compensation other than travel expenses for their efforts.

Finally, both for the committee and myself, I would like to express thanks to the staff for their commitment, dedication, and efforts. Bernard Michael, who served as study director, and Daniel Levine and Virginia Robinson, consultants, worked long and hard to provide a cohesive synthesis of our discussions, debates, and conclusions and rewrote patiently to accommodate us. The efforts of Eugenia Grohman, associate director of reports of the Commission on Behavioral and Social Sciences and Education, in editing the manuscript were especially valuable in preparing the report for publication. To Evelyn Simeon and Carole Foote, who served as administrative secretaries to the study, we also owe a well-deserved thanks. We and the volunteer community are indebted to them.

LEONARD BICKMAN, *Chair*
Committee on the Use of Volunteers in Schools

Contents

VOLUNTEERS IN PUBLIC SCHOOLS

1

Introduction

Americans have long prided themselves on an education system dedicated to extending knowledge to the broadest possible spectrum of children and youth. The participation of volunteers in furthering the education process is both perceived and believed to be good and to contribute to the welfare of America's students. Yet, given such widely held beliefs, surprisingly little is known about school-based volunteerism. Bits and pieces describing particular programs or activities abound, but not much is known about the overall picture.

In part to meet the needs for such information and in part to promote the concept of volunteerism, the U.S. Congress included a provision in the Higher Education Amendments of 1986 for a study to be conducted by the National Academy of Sciences on how volunteers can best be used in the classroom (Section 1341, P.L. 99-498). The study was carried out at the request of the U.S. Department of Education by a committee established under the Commission on Behavioral and Social Sciences and Education (CBASSE) of the National Research Council.

Despite increasing interest in using volunteers to enhance the education of American youths, attempts to study their contributions to pupils and teachers, to the schools, and to the community have been largely local studies focusing on specific projects. These data from local school districts and anecdotal information gathered by the committee suggested considerable growth in the numbers of volunteers over the past several decades. This was borne out to some extent by a 1985 study conducted by the Gallup organization for the Independent Sector, which showed an increase in volunteer participation in education of some 4 percent between 1981 and 1985, at the same time that overall volunteer activity was recording a decline of the same magnitude.

The pool from which school volunteers are drawn has changed according to school officials and others knowledgeable in this area. Twenty to 30 years ago most school volunteers were mothers of school children, but this source has been reduced as women have moved into paid employment. Increasingly, people from the business community, retired citizens, and college students have been actively recruited by school systems, and these groups now constitute a substantial portion of volunteers.

As the pool of school volunteers has become more diverse, so have the kinds of activities in which they engage. Growing public concern with the quality of education has resulted in greater emphasis on volunteering to help with activities directly related to student learning.

The committee found a great variety of services provided by volunteers, including: tutoring students in need of special help with such skills as reading, writing, and mathematics; listening attentively to children who "need a special friend"; working to develop English-language skills in children who are immigrants to the United States; acting as mentors and role models, and providing career guidance for disadvantaged youths; enhancing students' appreciation of arts and literature through lectures and demonstrations and helping in hands-on application of arts and crafts; organizing and operating computer labs; accompanying choral and other musical events; helping students organize science fairs, school newspapers, and dramatic events; and serving as guest lecturers on topics in which volunteers have experience and expertise. The committee also observed programs in which volunteers serve as surrogate grandparents in intergenerational programs that try to overcome stereotypical separations between young and old.

In addition to helping with instructional activities, large numbers of volunteers assist in libraries and media centers; help to monitor school lunch rooms and playgrounds; relieve teachers of paperwork and other nonacademic chores; help with field trips; and advise and support students in a wide range of clubs, competitions, and athletic events.

The literature reviewed as well as school officials and volunteer coordinators interviewed emphasize that the role of volunteers in all of these activities is to supplement rather than supplant professional school personnel. Their tasks are to augment and enrich the teaching and other activities in schools and classrooms. The committee learned of instances in which volunteers have become a bridge between schools and their communities, helping the communities to understand the schools' missions and needs.

Early in its study the committee became aware of the generally positive image attached to the concept of volunteerism. It was evident that the body of research on volunteers consists largely of specific studies on projects, such as tutoring and serving as mentors, plus informal evaluation studies based on teachers' or volunteers' perceptions as to the effectiveness of volunteer efforts. In its analysis of the literature and information from site visits and interviews, the committee was especially careful to approach the review critically and to attempt to draw reasonable conclusions as to the efficacy and value of volunteerism. Problem areas and possible negative aspects, as well as the positive, were considered in this review.

In conducting its study, the committee attempted to address questions such as: How large is the school volunteer effort? What is the number of schools, volunteers, teachers, and students involved? What is the nature of volunteer activities and how are they distributed? What is known about the contribution of school volunteers (for example, to increased academic achievement, to improved student attitudes, to teacher effectiveness, to community support for education)? What is known about factors that are important to the success of volunteer programs? Are there common elements among successful programs? What problems should schools anticipate in implementing a program to use volunteers in the classroom? What problems should volunteers expect?

The first task of the committee was to agree on a definition of a "school volunteer" in order to establish the scope and limits of the study. Volunteers interact with schools in many ways. Initially, the committee intended to focus on volunteer activities related only to students in the classroom. However, we discovered that these are difficult to isolate from clerical and other support activities in a school. Accordingly, we decided to consider the broader picture of the use of volunteers in public schools, from kindergarten through high school (grades K–12). Thus, the term "school (or classroom) volunteer" as used in this report generally refers to persons who work without pay, usually under the direction of an authorized teacher or other school employee, in support of school objectives to enhance the education of students. It includes people who participate in some aspect of instruction as well as those who help with clerical or other support activities. This definition with minor modifications in wording is used by the National Association of Partners in Education, the major professional organization with which directors of school volunteer services, volunteer coordinators, and volunteers are affiliated. Most state agencies that define the term also restrict it to unpaid service, as do most school districts.

Business-education partnerships, a rapidly growing area of community involvement in education, often provide financial or material gifts to schools, employment opportunities for teachers and students, and other forms of collaboration with schools. For this study, however, the committee considered only those business efforts that involve placement of volunteers in schools. Similarly, members of the Parent-Teacher Associations (PTAs), citizen activist organizations, advisory councils, or other parent or community groups connected with schools were not included unless they actually serve as school volunteers. It is recognized, however, that PTAs and other groups frequently are the major vehicle through which volunteers are recruited and that parent volunteers are often members of PTAs or other groups.

The term "unpaid" in every case refers to payment by the school system. Persons who are released by their employers on paid company time to work with schools are generally considered volunteers. Likewise, senior citizens or others who receive a small stipend when serving in the foster grandparents or similar programs are also included as volunteers. In analyzing available data and research findings, however, the committee could not always hold strictly to this definition. For example, we found that persons on advisory groups, high school or other K–12 students who serve as tutors or aides, and persons who volunteer in afterschool and Saturday programs are considered volunteers by some school districts but not by others.

Some of the bills under debate in the U.S. Congress during the course of this study would provide modest stipends for volunteers. For example, several of the national service bills under consideration in early 1989 would pay volunteers a minimum stipend and entitle them to an additional sum for schooling at the completion of their service. Although such legislation, if enacted, could make a big difference in the numbers and types of volunteers available to the schools, it would not affect our definition. Such volunteers would still provide unpaid services to schools, even though they would receive stipends from federal, state, or local governments.

In carrying out the study, the committee undertook four major tasks:

1. To create a profile or portrait of the use of volunteers in schools by assembling, organizing, and assessing available data and descriptions of volunteer programs in schools.

2. To assemble and analyze the research literature with respect to the contribution of volunteers. The main focus was on educational effects (student achievement, student attendance, student motivation and attitudes, and assistance to teachers), but economic contributions, effects on the volunteers themselves, and effects on the community were also reviewed. Negative effects (for example, administrative or teacher opposition) and their possible consequences were examined to the extent permitted by existing evidence.

3. To provide detailed descriptions of a small number of exemplary programs, based on site visits.

4. To examine and provide conclusions on the factors that foster or inhibit successful volunteer programs.

This report is the result of the committee's efforts. Chapter 2 presents a brief history of the organized volunteer movement. A profile or portrait, largely based on statistical data, of the use of volunteers comprises Chapter 3. Chapter 4 is an analysis of the literature on research and evaluation with respect to the use of volunteers in schools. In Chapter 5, we analyze the committee's 13 site visits to exemplary volunteer programs, including a description of the criteria by which the sites were chosen, the protocols followed, a discussion of each of the programs observed, and a summary of findings. The factors that the committee believes foster or inhibit successful programs are reviewed in Chapter 6, including a brief discussion of the findings from this study that might be helpful to the Congress as it considers possible legislation with respect to a national voluntary youth service program. Recommendations are included at the end of the chapters as appropriate. The report concludes with "A Call to Action," which presents the committee's conclusions and concerns, highlights elements of broad national interest, and proposes actions by the President, the Secretary of Education, and the Congress to support the use of volunteers in schools.

2

Development of Organized School Volunteerism in the United States

Although voluntary participation in many different areas of effort is woven throughout American history as a nation, school volunteerism as an organized effort to bring parents and other citizens into schools as unpaid aides is relatively recent. The story of this effort began in the 1950s, when a group of New York City civic activitists became concerned about the educational needs of children who entered school with the disadvantages of poverty, physical handicaps, or the inability to speak English.

When they began planning for an organized volunteer program, the New York City group knew of at least six other school districts in the country that used volunteers. They were also aware of work being done in England, where in London schools alone 2,500 volunteers were assisting in guidance and health services under a carefully organized plan. They also knew that principals in some elementary schools in New York City welcomed volunteers—usually parents or interested neighbors—on an informal basis, with no recruiting or training involved.

What the New York City citizens had in mind was a more structured and accountable volunteer activity that would recruit volunteers, provide training, and consult teachers about whether they wished to have volunteers in their classrooms. In 1956, the Public Education Association (PEA), a citizen advocacy group that had promoted education in New York City for half a century, led an organized school volunteer program with 20 volunteers who offered their services on a regular weekly basis at P.S. 191 in Manhattan to tutor children in reading. From the beginning, the program emphasized that the volunteers would be trained.

The program flourished in the pilot school, and requests for volunteers came to the PEA from other schools. In 1959, the Ford Foundation granted $80,000 to the PEA to expand the school volunteer program. It was understood that the grant would also be used to improve recruitment, training, and utilization of volunteers and that over the 3-year period of the grant the New York City Board of Education would pick up an increasing share of the cost of the program. The PEA also received financial support for its volunteer initiative from the New York Fund for Children, the Eda K. Loeb Foundation, and the Mary W. Harriman Fund.

As word of the New York City program spread, the PEA received more requests than it could handle for advice and help with setting up similar programs in other school districts around the country. In 1964, it asked for and received another 3-year grant from the Ford Foundation to create a National School Volunteer Program under the PEA umbrella.

Under the grant, the PEA agreed to assist citizen groups in about 20 large cities to train school volunteers, using the methods that had been successful in New York City. The PEA added to its staff in order to provide consultant services and conduct workshops in the designated cities and to prepare training materials. Ultimately, 17 large cities received assistance from the PEA in creating or expanding school volunteer programs: Baltimore, Boston, Chicago, Cincinnati, Cleveland, Detroit, Los Angeles, Milwaukee, New Orleans, New York, Philadelphia, Pittsburgh, San Diego, San Francisco, Seattle, St. Louis, and Washington, D.C.

Buoyed by the success of the National School Volunteer Program, a group of advocates approached the Ford Foundation in 1968 to ask for support for a School Volunteer Program that could become self-sustaining. Ford responded with a 1-year grant for the creation of an independent National School Volunteer Program (NSVP). The new NSVP, now incorporated as the National School Volunteer Program, Inc., established an office in New York City.

After the expiration of the Ford Foundation grant in 1969, the NSVP closed its national office, and for a number of years it operated from the school district of the person then serving as president. The organization continued to convene national meetings, provide technical assistance to new programs, and facilitate the exchange of information between volunteer programs in school districts around the country. In 1975, a planning grant from the Edna McConnell Clark Foundation to the National School Volunteer Program, Inc., enabled it to make plans for a new national office. The following year, 1976, with additional grants from the Clark Foundation, NSVP opened a national office with an executive director and a small staff in Alexandria, Virginia.

There were other developments in school volunteerism in this period. In 1970, the Office of Education, then part of the U.S. Department of Health, Education, and Welfare, created an Office of Volunteers in Education in the Bureau of Education Professions Development. The creation of this volunteer office was sparked in part by the surprising national response to a speech by Commissioner of Education James Allen describing a concept called "Right to Read," which was to have a strong volunteer component. A corps of energetic supporters of Right to Read, many of them volunteers, staffed the office in its first months, helping to answer the large volume of mail generated by Allen's proposal.

The Office of Volunteers in Education began with modest funding of $100,000 from three vocational education programs; the office eventually received almost $1 million from several other federal education programs. During its 2-year life, it supported programs to train school volunteer coordinators at the Washington Technical Institute in the District of Columbia and in Des Moines, Iowa, and convened a number of conferences. In addition, the office encouraged the states to set up contacts for volunteer programs. However, this office was only a very small operation, and after 2 years it was eliminated during a reorganization of the Office of Education.

That same year, 1972, the Institute for Development of Educational Activities, Inc. (IDEA), an affiliate of the Charles F. Kettering Foundation, convened a national seminar in Melbourne, Florida, to ascertain the status of volunteers in the matter of teaching and learning as well as to determine the roadblocks to their expanded use. A report on the seminar characterized school volunteerism as a "proliferating activity" and stressed that the volunteer movement in education is a true grass-roots phenomenon at the time (Institute for Development of Educational Activities, Inc., [IDEA], 1972).

Most of the people attending the seminar were coordinators of local school volunteer programs; they came from San Francisco, California; Winnetka, Illinois; Boston, Massachusetts; New Orleans, Louisiana; Los Angeles, California; Englewood, New Jersey; Tulsa, Oklahoma; Kansas City, Missouri; Houston, Texas; Worcester, Massachusetts; and the state of New Hampshire. Also present were the vice-president for education of the National Association of Manufacturers and representatives of several community colleges, the American Red Cross, and the National Center for Voluntary Action in Washington, D.C.

Seminar attendees confined themselves to discussing volunteers as direct participants in the education process. The report (IDEA, 1972) on the seminar gives considerable attention to volunteers as a way of reducing the ratio of students to adults in classrooms and a way of giving students individual, one-to-one attention. In providing services such as tutoring to students in need of help, volunteers might really be "teaching," the report noted, though conference attendees acknowledged that the word "reinforcing" is more palatable to professional educators.

The conferees noted that volunteer programs sometimes started as the idea of a superintendent or school board member or as a small effort put together by a teacher or principal; more often, dedicated groups have to demonstrate and justify the program before they can get the institutional interest and backing. Major roadblocks to school volunteer programs were school administrators, shy and insecure teachers, and teacher unions. The report laid a great deal of the blame and responsibility for teachers' fear of volunteers at the door of teacher-training institutions, which do not enlighten the novice teacher that anyone else in the community could possibly be of any help.

Participants in the 1972 seminar cited the need for:

an independent national organization in order to give cohesiveness to the multitudinous programs proliferating at the local level. . . . We need to have some kind of dissemination of information so that others will know what is going on, where things are happening, where new developments are taking place, and how a group of volunteers can improve their own program. . . . The volunteer effort needs an agency for dissemination, technical assistance, some kind of regular moral and, possibly, financial support. This does not mean government support, as the program will be far stronger if it is nongovernmental in nature.

During the 1970s and continuing in the 1980s, school volunteer programs sprang up in many towns and cities around the country, often spontaneously, sparked by interest and enthusiasm on the part of an individual parent, teacher, or school principal. The national organization provided support to the emerging programs in the form of conferences, newsletters, and training manuals and other materials.

In some communities, school desegregation spurred the volunteer movement. During the 1970s and continuing into the 1980s, school systems, first in the South and then in the North, faced new problems of pupil and teacher assignment, busing, and curriculum improvement as the result of voluntary or court-ordered desegregation plans. In some cities, parents and other volunteers rallied to prove the worth of public schools by offering their services in a variety of roles, including classroom support and public relations.

The growing community schools movement was also a stimulus to volunteerism. "Community education," generally defined as opening schools to a variety of community activities, encouraged community members to think of themselves as participants in the education process, and many became volunteers in the schools.

But nothing focused attention on education more than a series of critical reports that began in 1983 with publication of the U.S. Department of Education's *A Nation at Risk*, which noted many deficiencies in the education children were receiving in the United States. The effect of this and a series of other critiques was two-way: citizens became more interested in what schools were doing, and educators looked for ways to bring allies into the schools, to help with services and to bolster community support.

In 1988, NSVP reported that school volunteer programs were active in all 50 states, the District of Columbia, and the U.S. territories.

One of the major initiatives to emerge from the heightened public awareness of education and education-related problems in the 1980s was a variety of cooperative arrangements between schools and businesses or other community agencies, often in the form of partnerships or school adoptions, aimed at improving the quality of education and better preparing students to compete as workers in a world economy. In 1988, NSVP merged with the National Symposium on Partnerships in Education to form the National Association of Partners in Education.

Two other organizations have made major contributions to volunteerism in schools. One is the national PTA, founded in 1897 as the National Congress of Mothers, with the threefold purpose of educating and involving parents in better rearing their own children, providing needed services to all children, and strengthening support for public education. Currently, with 6.5 million members, the national PTA calls itself the largest voluntary organization in the United States. Its members, predominantly but not exclusively parents of school children, are committed to improving the lives and education of all children, not just their own, through service and advocacy. In many schools, the local PTA is the major source of school volunteers. PTAs also support schools through fund raising and contribution of equipment and facilities.

Another organization that has played a significant role in school volunteerism is the Junior League, a national organization of women committed to community service. Local leagues are grouped in an umbrella Association of Junior Leagues headquartered in New York City. Since its inception in 1921, the league has been active in education. Junior leaguers work as volunteers in many schools, and the league has initiated and financially supported many volunteer activities. A major contribution of the league has been the development of education curricula specifically designed to use volunteers in a variety of school activities, including enrichment for gifted and talented children, aid in improving reading and other skills for disadvantaged youngsters, and supplementary programs in science, mathematics, and reading.

Local junior leagues have autonomy to develop volunteer activities responsive to the needs of their local schools. The Association of Junior Leagues provides technical support and assistance to local leagues and has developed national programs that use volunteers to address a range of education-related problems, including drug abuse and teenage pregnancy.

This brief account of the development of organized school volunteerism in the United States is necessarily incomplete. It does not include the varied experiences of school districts around the country that were developing volunteer programs at the time the events recorded here occurred. It does not attempt to relate the school volunteer movement to other historical developments, such as the enactment of federal education legislation, or increased acceptance by teacher unions of paid auxiliary aides in classrooms. Nor does it attempt to look at school volunteerism in the context of other major developments, such as the pressures on educators in recent years to welcome community involvement in schools as a means of school improvement or public relations. The varied experiences of school districts around the country developing volunteer programs at the time the events recorded here were occurring should also be part of any history of the use of volunteers in schools. Some of these experiences are described in the chapter on exemplary volunteer programs, but these also are only part of the story. This brief synopsis is intended to provide some context for understanding the development of organized school volunteers programs in the United States; the comprehensive history is yet to be written.

REFERENCE

Institute for Development of Education Activities, Inc. (IDEA)
　1972　*Expanding Volunteers in Teching and Learning Programs.* Dayton, Ohio: Institute for Development of Educational Activities, Inc.

3

School Volunteers:
A Statistical Profile

INTRODUCTION

Although wide attention is being paid to the importance of unpaid volunteers and their contributions to the educational process, surprisingly little of a current or reliable nature is known about the size of this group of people, its composition, its distribution, or the breadth of its activities. Most studies conducted in the past have dealt with a very broad scope of volunteerism; thus, the ability to extract information solely on volunteers in schools, and especially on activities contributing to the educational process, has been severely limited. In addition, the variety and looseness of the definitions used have made it difficult to develop comparisons between various studies. And other studies have only a few items devoted to volunteer activity in the schools, providing limited useful information. Thus, in developing the profile of volunteers in this chapter, we used, as much as possible, data from a variety of sources. The main source, however, was the data provided by the U.S. Department of Education's National Center for Education Statistics (NCES).

The committee has been most fortunate that its work coincided with the efforts of the NCES to produce current and reliable information on teachers, school administrators, and school policies and practices. To meet the need for information on the critical aspects of teacher supply and demand, the composition of the administrator and teacher work force, and the general status of teaching and schooling, NCES mounted an integrated survey covering the 1987–1988 school year; it involved seven different inquiries to schools, school districts, principals, and teachers, in both public and private sectors. The sample for the 1987 effort consists of

9,300 public and 3,500 private schools throughout the 50 states. Two of the seven surveys—those addressed to public and private schools—each contain two questions on the use of unpaid volunteers. Responses were obtained from 90 percent of the public schools and 70 percent of the private schools. The questions were similar to those included by NCES in a study of public schools conducted during the 1984–1985 school year (and one of private schools conducted in 1985–1986) and, thus, for the first time, some comparisons of changes over time are possible. It should be emphasized, however, that the data in this report from the 1987–1988 survey are preliminary; corrections may be forthcoming, as well as adjustments for nonresponse; when these data are published by the center in the near future, slight differences may be expected. Preliminary data from the 1987–1988 NCES surveys are presented in Appendix A.

It is important to note that the questions used in both the 1987–1988 and earlier surveys are prospective in nature, asking an administrator to estimate how many volunteers the school expects and will use during the full school year that has just begun. For the 1987–1988 survey, the questions were as follows:

> Do any UNPAID VOLUNTEERS provide services for this school? Do not include students from this school as unpaid volunteers.
>
> How many unpaid volunteers do you expect will perform services at this school on a CONTINUING OR SCHEDULED BASIS during the 1987–1988 school year?

Furthermore, the forms were not accompanied by instructions defining the terms, thus leaving interpretations of the questions to the respondent. Accordingly, the numbers entered by the school staff may reflect a wide variety of different influences, such as the experience of the previous school year, expectations based on the new school year, hopes and aspirations rather than reality, the desire to see a stated goal accomplished, or a misinterpretation of the questions. In the absence of any evaluation to measure the extent to which the guesstimate deviates from the actual use of volunteers during the year, the numbers must be viewed with appropriate caution. Nonetheless, results from these two surveys provide the best and most consistent basis at this time for comparing the use of unpaid volunteers in schools.

Several comments about some statistical aspects of surveys should be noted. The estimates presented in this chapter are mostly derived from samples and as such are subject to sampling variability. The measure of variation due to sampling (the estimated standard error of a statistic) provides an indication of the precision of the estimates derived from the sample. Estimates derived from the studies conducted by NCES generally have relatively small standard errors, and the reports issued by NCES present examples of standard errors for a number of representative statistics. Thus, when NCES publishes final results of the 1987–1988 study, measures of sampling error will be included. Similarly, reports containing data from the 1985 survey will present measures of error. When such information was readily available for the other studies cited in this chapter, it is noted in the text.

The reliability of estimates is directly related to the number of cases in a cell, and caution should be exercised in the interpretation of figures based on a relatively small number of cases, as well as in the interpretation of small differences between estimates. If the questionnaires had been completed by different respondents, the responses would have been different; some numbers might have been higher, while others might have been lower.

The data also reflect the effects of nonsampling problems, such as the failure of some respondents to reply to the questionnaire, misunderstanding on the part of respondents as to the proper meaning of the questions, failure to answer all of the questions, errors in coding or processing the results, or failure to adhere to the specifications in carrying out the survey. These sources of error also affect the reliability of the results. Generally, no allowance is made in this chapter for these sources of error.

THE NATIONAL PICTURE

Some 1.3 million people were expected to participate as school volunteers in the school year beginning in the fall of 1987, according to preliminary information prepared by NCES from the Schools and Staffing Surveys conducted in the fall of 1987: about 1 million people were expected to contribute their time to the public schools, and an additional 295,000 unpaid volunteers were expected in private schools. The 1987 figure for volunteers in public schools is not substantially different from the 1.1 million reported by NCES for 1985; the figure for volunteers in private schools at the current time, however, is almost three times the 1985 figure of 100,000. Volunteers were found in about 47,300, or 60 percent, of the nation's elementary and secondary public schools; the comparable figure for private schools was 17,700, or 65 percent of all private schools.

The remainder of this discussion describes the public school sector, which was the focus of the charge to the committee (see Table 3-1). However, when available, data are presented for private schools (see Table 3-2).

The expected use of volunteers varied widely between schools in the

1987–1988 school year. For example, in schools with small enrollments (fewer than 150 students), about 40 percent reported no volunteers, and the 60 percent that reported the use of unpaid volunteers averaged about seven volunteers per school. At the other extreme, about 75 percent of schools with more than 500 students reported the use of volunteers, and they averaged close to 30 volunteers per school. There is greater use of volunteers at the elementary level: volunteers are found at 75 percent of elementary schools, and there are an average of about 24 volunteers per school; at the middle and secondary school levels just over 50 percent report the use of volunteers, with an average of about 15 volunteers per school.

Public schools with high minority enrollment (50 percent or more) were less likely to use volunteers and reported fewer on average than did schools with lower minority enrollment. Close to 50 percent of the minority schools reported no volunteers, and those with volunteers indicated an average of about 15 volunteers per school; by comparison, about 30 percent of schools with less than 50 percent minority enrollment reported no volunteers, and those with volunteers average about 22 volunteers per school. This same relationship holds when the use of volunteers is examined by the composition of the teaching staff. Of schools with less than 20 percent minority teaching staff, 75 percent reported using volunteers and averaged about 22 volunteers per school; of the schools with 50 percent or greater minority teaching staff, less than 50 percent used volunteers, and the average was about 17 volunteers per school.

There are a number of possible explanations for these findings. Schools with high proportions of minority enrollment generally are located in areas whose residents have relatively low incomes. As a result, parents may be less likely to have either the time or the energy to engage in volunteer activity; there may be fewer intact families and fewer parents overall to participate; and there may be less understanding in such areas of the need for and importance of providing volunteer services. Whatever the cause of the imbalance, it is quite clear that children in such schools have less opportunity to receive any of the benefits that can be obtained from volunteer help. It also can be suggested that the possible benefits of school volunteers to children in such areas, in fact, would be much greater than in other areas or circumstances, given their probably greater needs.

Geographically, 70 percent of public schools in the West used volunteers and they also had the highest average number of volunteers, almost 27 per school. Just over 50 percent of schools in the South reported the use of volunteers, with an average of 23 volunteers per school. In the northeast and north central regions, 65 percent and 75 percent used volunteers, respectively; both regions reported an average of 16 volunteers per school.

TABLE 3-1 Public Schools with Volunteers, 1987–1988, by Selected Characteristics

Category	Total Schools	Total Volunteers	Average Number of Volunteers per School
Total	47,302	1,015,442	21.5
Enrollment			
Less than 150	3,167	21,659	6.8
150–299	7,337	84,368	11.5
300–499	14,516	281,418	19.4
500–749	11,072	329,952	30.0
More than 750	7,342	194,383	26.5
NA/NR	55	426	7.7
Minority Enrollment			
Less than 5 percent	14,255	254,425	17.8
5–19 percent	11,042	299,843	27.2
20–49 percent	8,471	199,674	23.6
50–74 percent	4,187	72,187	17.2
More than 75 percent	4,865	72,454	14.9
NA/NR	671	13,623	20.3
Minority Teachers			
Less than 5 percent	20,970	404,287	19.3
5–19 percent	10,944	284,684	26.0
20–49 percent	6,499	129,458	20.0
50–74 percent	2,064	35,703	17.3
More than 75 percent	989	14,053	14.2
NA/NR	2,024	44,021	21.8
Type of School			
Elementary	31,198	739,144	23.7
Middle/junior	5,031	71,668	14.2
Secondary	3,820	61,230	16.0
Combined	1,865	18,864	10.1
Other	1,557	21,180	13.6
NA/NR	18	121	6.6
Type of Community			
Rural/farming	12,123	140,881	11.6
Town[a]	10,902	210,479	19.3
Suburban	8,474	270,323	31.9
Urban	11,529	285,462	24.8
Other	324	4,112	12.7
NA/NR	138	950	6.9

TABLE 3-1 (Continued)

Category	Total Schools	Total Volunteers	Average Number of Volunteers per School
Region			
North Central	12,254	194,618	15.9
Northeast	6,369	104,661	16.4
South	14,798	341,641	23.1
West	10,069	271,287	27.0

[a]Less than 50,000 population.

NA/NR: Data not available or not reported.

NOTE: The totals reflect an adjustment for survey nonresponse. The details, however, have not been adjusted to reflect nonresponse, either to the full survey or to a specific characteristic. Accordingly, the details do not add to the totals and differ somewhat among tables.

SOURCE: Unpublished data from the U.S. Department of Education.

Rural areas and small towns had the smallest number of volunteers, fewer than 20 on average; suburban areas turned out the largest number, about 32 volunteers per school. The average for urban schools was 25 volunteers per school.

The results from this most recent study confirm the widespread use of volunteers in public schools. Irrespective of school size or location, and irrespective of the makeup or mixture of student bodies or teaching staff, volunteers evidently are viewed and accepted as a useful component of the education process. Nonetheless, variations in the use of volunteers do exist, as noted above. Overall, about 25 percent of all elementary schools and more than 50 percent of all middle and secondary schools report no use of volunteers. The implications of these differences should be examined. Studies should be undertaken to provide understanding and guidance as to why some schools use volunteers and others do not, as well as to how volunteer programs can be improved.

Unfortunately, the latest NCES study did not obtain information on the activities of volunteers. To offset this limitation to some extent, we have used results from the 1985 study, which did include such information (see Table 3-3). Those results show that the major focus of volunteer activity in the public schools, occupying almost 40 percent of all volunteers, was in the area of instructional support, such as tutoring, grading papers, monitoring in science laboratories, conducting rote exercises, and the like. The next most reported activity, involving about 30 percent of volunteers,

TABLE 3-2   Private Schools with Volunteers, 1987–1988, by Selected
Characteristics

Category	Total Schools	Total Volunteers	Average Number of Volunteers per School
Total	17,738	345,994	19.5
Enrollment			
Less than 150	6,253	43,714	7.0
150–299	4,650	87,289	18.8
300–499	1,898	54,525	28.7
500–749	782	27,117	34.7
More than 750	356	17,564	49.4
NA/NR			
Minority Enrollment			
Less than 5 percent	6,433	115,143	17.9
5–19 percent	4,175	61,877	14.8
20–49 percent	1,627	27,829	17.1
50–74 percent	594	14,698	24.8
More than 75 percent	923	5,917	6.4
NA/NR	188	4,744	25.3
Minority Teachers			
Less than 5 percent	9,900	170,762	17.2
5–19 percent	2,149	39,950	18.6
20–49 percent	759	6,770	8.9
50–74 percent	291	1,390	4.8
More than 75 percent	223	1,622	7.3
NA/NR	616	9,713	15.8
Type of School			
Elementary	8,653	146,103	16.9
Middle/junior	178	1,998	11.2
Secondary	855	23,727	27.8
Combined	2,434	35,423	14.6
Other	1,817	22,947	12.6
NA/NR	1	10	10.0
Type of Community			
Rural/farming	2,329	22,373	9.6
Town[a]	3,597	51,132	14.2
Suburban	2,777	62,202	22.4
Urban	5,198	94,189	18.1
Other	6	214	35.0
NA/NR	33	99	3.3

TABLE 3-2 (Continued)

Category	Total Schools	Total Volunteers	Average Number of Volunteers per School
Region			
North Central	5,234	79,239	15.1
Northeast	3,241	54,821	16.9
South	2,943	39,533	13.4
West	2,521	56,615	22.5
Religious Orientation			
Secular	1,529	21,284	13.9
Religious	12,366	208,690	16.9
NA	44	234	5.3
Catholic	6,788	155,652	22.9
Other religious	5,570	52,852	9.5
NA	1,581	21,704	13.7

[a]Less than 50,000 population.

NA/NR: Data not available or not reported.

NOTE: The totals reflect an adjustment for survey nonresponse. The details, however, have not been adjusted to reflect nonresponse, either to the full survey or to a specific characteristic. Accordingly, the details do not add to the totals and differ somewhat among tables.

SOURCE: Unpublished data from the U.S. Department of Education.

was extracurricular support in athletics, clubs, trips, newspapers, and libraries. Just under 15 percent of voluneers provided management or advisory support, such as a citizen advisory group organized through the school; around 10 percent gave clerical support to the school, while a similar proportion worked at monitoring the cafeteria or playground. Less than 5 percent of volunteers assisted in the area of guidance support, such as career and college counseling or in health and drug awareness.[1]

At the elementary school level, just under 50 percent of the volunteers were involved with instructional support activities, followed by extracurricular and advisory support activities. In contrast, at the secondary school level, extracurricular support was the main task of volunteers, involving just under 50 percent of all volunteers, followed by advisory support func-

[1]The numbers add to more than 100 percent because some volunteers contribute to more than one activity.

TABLE 3-3 Volunteers in Public Schools, 1984–1985, by Activity

Activity	All Schools		Elementary Schools		Secondary Schools	
	Number	Percent	Number	Percent	Number	Percent
Instructional support	473,476	43.5	448,217	44.8	29,259	15.4
Guidance support	50,383	4.6	36,765	3.6	13,617	8.3
Extracurricular support	301,749	27.7	234,844	23.5	66,856	40.8
Management/ advisory	147,540	13.6	109,234	10.9	38,306	23.4
Clerical support	102,975	9.5	88,082	8.8	14,886	9.1
Other support	94,831	8.7	83,106	8.3	11,726	7.2

NOTE: Percentages add to more than total because of multiple activities.
SOURCE: Unpublished data from the U.S. Department of Education.

tions (occupying about 25 percent of the volunteers), and instructional support, in which about 12 percent of volunteers participated.

Instructional support was the main area in which volunteers assisted in the West, involving almost 60 percent of the volunteers, compared with about 40 percent elsewhere in the nation. The West used fewer volunteers in both extracurricular and clerical support, areas in which the rest of the country use large proportions of their volunteers.

A major drawback of the current NCES effort to obtain information on the school volunteer universe is that it fails to provide any demographic data about the people who serve as volunteers. To provide some understanding of this important area, we have used a study conducted by the Gallup organization in fall 1985 for the Independent Sector, a public nonprofit coalition of corporate, foundation, and voluntary organizations established to assist the voluntary sector (see Independent Sector, 1986). The information was obtained through personal interviews with a national sample of 1,638 respondents 14 years of age and older. The report notes that major findings have a sampling tolerance of plus or minus 3 percent.

According to Gallup, about 13 percent of the population 14 years of age and over reported some volunteer work in education during the previous year, about the same as in 1981. However, a fall to 8 percent was reported when the question was restricted to volunteer activity in the previous month. A majority of the volunteers had contributed 4 or less hours during a week. It should be noted that "volunteer work" in this survey included any and all activities involving education, whether public or private, fund raising, teaching Sunday school, or adult education.

Although separate data are not available from the Gallup surveys on the characteristics of those contributing their time and efforts to education, it is informative to examine the characteristics of all volunteers, with a very broad assumption of general similarity (see Table 3-4). In fall 1985, about 48 percent of the population 14 years old or over reported volunteer activity of all kinds over a 12-month period (about the same proportion as reported in a study conducted for the Rockefeller Brothers Fund in 1985). The Gallup study showed that 50 percent of women had engaged in some volunteer activity, compared with 45 percent of men. The participation rate was relatively constant up to age 50, about 50 percent, at which point it fell to around 40 percent. Whites were much more likely to have volunteered than blacks (49 percent compared with 38 percent), and the higher the educational attainment, the more likely the person was to have engaged in volunteer activity—the percentage rose from 29 percent of those with a grade school education to a high of 65 percent for those with 4 or more years of college. The same relationship held for income—those with family incomes of $30,000 or more were half again as likely to participate in volunteer activity as were those with family incomes below that level. These data also suggest a major change that took place during the post-World War II period in the functions undertaken by volunteers with respect to schools, that is, away from fund raising and school mother activities to assisting teachers and schools in the fundamental task of educating children.

There was an effort to profile volunteers in public schools in 1981–1982, when the National School Volunteer Program (NSVP) surveyed a national sample of school districts. Unfortunately, a history of this survey, including survey procedures, specific instructions, response rates, estimating methodology, tabulation specifications, and results is not available. However, an unpublished two-page summary of results provides the following reported findings:

- More than 4.4 million persons provided part- or full-time volunteer services to public schools over a 12-month period in 1981–1982.
- Each volunteer contributed an average of about 3 hours per week.
- Volunteers were found in 79 percent of public school districts.
- Volunteer services were used more extensively at the elementary level; volunteers were found in 88 percent of the elementary schools and in 60 percent of the secondary schools.
- Volunteers were parents, 33 percent; older citizens, 24 percent; students, 21 percent; business employees, 18 percent; and other, 4 percent.

TABLE 3-4   All Volunteers in Past 12 Months, by
Selected Characteristics, March 1981 and October 1985
(in percent)

Characteristics	March 1981	October 1985
Total	52	48
Sex		
Male	47	45
Female	56	51
Age		
14–17	53	52
18–24	54	43
25–34	NA	53
25–64	55	51
35–49	NA	54
50–64	NA	44
65 and older	37	38
65–74	NA	43
75 and older	NA	26
Race		
White	54	49
Black and other races	41	38
Marital status		
Married	53	52
Single	58	39
Divorced/separated/widowed	42	39
Employment		
Full-time	55	49
Part-time	65	62
Not employed	45	44
Education		
Grade school	26	29
Some high school	31	38
Four-year high school	54	46
College, less than 4 years	65	61
College, 4 or more years	75	65

TABLE 3-4   (Continued)

Characteristics	March 1981	October 1985
Income		
Under $10,000	36	40
$10,000–$19,000	49	42
$20,000–$29,000	NA	44
$20,000–$39,000	64	52
$30,000–$39,000	NA	64
$40,000–$49,000	NA	67
More than $40,000	62	60
Region		
East	51	43
Midwest	54	52
South	48	44
West	57	54

NA: Not available.

SOURCE: Independent Sector (1986: Table 1).

A few words of caution are in order concerning these data. As noted earlier, details on the conduct of this study are lacking. Furthermore, unlike the NCES surveys that were directed to a sample of schools, this survey used a school-district-level sample to obtain data on the use of volunteers in schools in the district. This sampling procedure is considered less reliable than a school-based sample because school districts are often less likely to be able to respond with reasonably accurate data. Finally, we were informed that only about one-half of the sampled school districts responded, and nonrespondents were not followed up; it was thus assumed that the number and distribution of volunteers in school districts that did not reply were similar to those that did. If, as is usually the case, school districts that did reply were far more likely to have volunteers than those that did not respond, serious overestimates of the total number of volunteers may have resulted.

We also note that the approach used more recently by NCES to measure the universe of volunteers in schools results in a number far less than the 4.4 million reported in the NSVP study. It strains credibility to assume that the level of participation has fallen precipitously in the intervening period, particularly since anecdotal information and data from the committee's site visits, especially those in big cities, indicated growth rather than decline in the participation of volunteers in schools.

For these reasons, we cast a doubtful eye on the 4.4 million figure, notwithstanding its wide use in the literature and folklore about the size of the volunteer effort in public schools. At the same time, we would note that those involved in the conduct of the NSVP survey did seek out competent professional advice, certainly as concerns the methodology of sample selection and sample size.

A later effort to obtain statistics on school volunteers, as already noted, was undertaken by the NCES in connection with its 1985 Public School Survey. The NCES questionnaire, addressed to the school administrator, included a single item: "Do any unpaid volunteers provide services for this school?" A "yes" response resulted in a request to enter the numbers of such volunteers. A similar study, which also included a question on the use of volunteers, was carried out a year later among private schools.

The public school survey in 1985 was conducted by mail for a national representative sample of 2,801 public schools and had a response rate of 84.6 percent. The sample size for the private school survey in 1986 was 1,387 private schools, with a response rate of just under 85 percent. No instructions or definitions of terms were provided; thus, the interpretation as to what constitutes an "unpaid volunteer" and the definition of "services" were left to the discretion of the respondent. The survey also had the drawback that a single total was not obtained; rather, administrators were asked to provide detail by the type of support provided. Because volunteers frequently engaged in more than one activity, there certainly is the possibility of some duplication. Despite these reservations, the results based on this survey—that public schools were using or planned to use some 1,088,230 volunteers in the 1984–1985 school year—are likely much closer to reality than the 4.4 million estimate of the NSVP summary.

Again, either in using or in musing about the significance of the data presented throughout this chapter, it is important both to note and to remember the caveats that attach to them. First, a time series based on a consistent and iterative data collection system does not yet exist, although the two most recent studies by NCES give promise in this direction. Prior estimates bore little or no relationship to one another—most notably, one that provided a measure of 4.4 million and the more recent one that estimated the total number of volunteers in public schools at 1.1 million.

Second, none of the measures to date has provided the potential respondent with a written definition of a volunteer, one that can stand both scrutiny and the test of time and that can be responded to easily and quickly. Nor has the definition of volunteer been standardized such that the list of activities to be included or excluded is clearly delineated, with agreement by those representing the schools that the components are reasonable and acceptable and can be isolated or separated, as desired. Third, even assuming a standard definition of volunteer, the numbers themselves are open to serious question. For example, during our visits to schools, we became aware that in some instances the counts of volunteers are derived by summing the names entered in the sign-in registers. In its brief exploration, the committee also became aware of instances in which the registers were incomplete, were not used at all, or contained duplicate, partial, or incomplete entries. And many schools, even given relatively good registers, do not bother to tally; rather, they choose a "typical" period—a day or week—and use the single tally as the guide for the entire school year. Based on the committee's observations, so-called knowledgeable estimates would appear to be a major source of the number of volunteers. As noted above, the committee also has reservations about the prospective nature of the questions now being used by NCES; we strongly urge the application of cognitive research in the development and testing of appropriate question wording, as well as the evaluation of results.

Taken together, these concerns lead to an overriding need for agreement on periodic collection of relevant, important, and much needed national information on the state of voluntary activity in schools. In this regard, we have in mind the regular collection of data both on the extent of voluntary activity and on the characteristics of those giving and receiving the unpaid services, that is, data collected both from schools and from the population of volunteers. The NCES has made a good beginning in collecting limited data from schools; it should now consider how frequently such information is to be collected and, more important, how and how much to expand the detail to be collected.

Similarly, NCES should review the need for information on the characteristics of school volunteers and determine the scope and frequency of what data to collect and how best to do so. The committee suggests that NCES consider a periodic supplement with rotating subject areas, which might be appended to the Current Population Survey conducted by the Bureau of the Census. Such an approach might provide an efficient, economical, and timely means of meeting needs for such data.

It is clear that standards on how the data should be gathered and evaluated must be established, agreed upon, and carried out. Furthermore, if individual states wish to collect such information—and a number of the states already do—they should be encouraged to use agreed-upon definitions and question wordings in order to ensure conformity with the national data. Above all, the responsibility for providing national data should and must rest with the federal government, in this case with NCES, which is legislatively charged to provide the Congress with information on the state of education. In our judgment, such an assessment must include information on the use of volunteers in schools.

The committee is not in a position to discuss who should be responsible for ensuring conformity and coordination among those concerned with and interested in this data collection effort.   Instead, we merely note with some emphasis the need for such action to be taken and suggest that the Secretary of Education provide the needed leadership in this area.

THE STATE PICTURE

Since education is primarily a state responsibility, it is not surprising that a number of states have active statewide volunteer programs. What is surprising, however, is that so many states seem to have so little in the way of legislation, leadership, or information about such programs. To obtain some information on the extent of states' roles, the committee sent a questionnaire to the states, extra-state jurisdictions, and the U.S. Department of Defense schools. Most of the state replies indicated great interest in community involvement in education; some even sent anecdotal information on the use of volunteers in their schools; a few suggested that they were about to move forward with both legislation and leadership; some referenced a variety of data collected, compiled, or otherwise composed at the local level; however, few had much of any substance to offer or display as their own contributions. If the 40 replies received are representative, it appears that local school districts and individual schools are far ahead of their state leadership.

This is surprising in view of the strong support by the Council of Chief State School Officers for parent, business, and other community involvement in education, including school volunteer partnership development. For example, the published policy statement of the council, a nonprofit organization comprised of the public officials responsible for education in each state, includes the following in regard to the use of school volunteers (Council of Chief State School Officers, 1988):

Volunteers provide vital assistance to educators and students in the reinforcement and enrichment of instruction and in the provision of related support services. Organized volunteer programs promote the involvement of a wide spectrum of the population including parents, business and industry personnel, community organization members, retirees and students.

The Council encourages state education agencies to provide leadership in working with local schools and communities to promote the statewide development of partnerships between professional educators and citizen volunteers to improve school effectiveness and student performance.

The National Association of State Boards of Education, the policy-making bodies in most states, has also issued statements encouraging citizen involvement in schools.

Nevertheless, only 14 of the states that replied to the committee's questions had enacted legislation or issued state board of education policy statements that authorized and encouraged the use of volunteers in schools.

An additional 27 indicated that they had "some kind" of program encouraging school districts to use volunteers, despite a lack of specific legislation or written policy, but they failed to provide any detail. Several noted that they do provide some financial or technical support but again did not provide any specific information. About half of the replies provided the name and address of a person at the state level who had been designated as responsible for school volunteer program coordination, and a small number provided a brief description of the responsibilities of the position.

The state of Florida has what is probably the strongest legislative commitment, with annual categorical funding for matching grants to school districts to promote and extend school volunteer programs. This program has resulted, according to statistics issued by the state for the 1987–1988 school year, in volunteer programs in more than 2,000 schools with more than 140,000 volunteers.

Another area of inquiry dealt with the availability of information at the state level on the extent of participation in public school voluntary activities and the characteristics of participants. Of the states that responded, some 16 indicated an availability of some information, but less than half of these provided information sufficient to support their contention or to enable the committee to evaluate their data. For example, one state noted in passing that the count of volunteers was not restricted to those who gave services in schools but, rather, included anyone who gave any service to the cause of education, anywhere in the state. Accordingly, this state reported five times as many volunteers as another state with a population that was eight times larger. In another instance, one state reported 23,000 volunteers contributed 5 million hours of effort (or 200 hours per volunteer), while another state with almost six times as many volunteers (140,900) showed only 6 million hours spent in service (or 43 hours per volunteer). Only two states reported having undertaken any kind of evaluation study.

A number of the states also attempted to quantify in dollar terms the value of the efforts of volunteers. As a first step, using sign-in records, observation, or assumed knowledge, the states developed an estimate of the average number of hours that volunteers devoted to the schools. They then ascribed an hourly dollar value to the aggregate number of hours, which produced an estimate of the overall dollar value. This approach also was followed in a number of the early data-gathering efforts: for example, the 1982 NSVP study estimated the value of volunteer services at "about $655 million." Even accepting the possible usefulness of such information, it is important to recognize that such figures are fraught with potential error which, on the one extreme, may reflect merely poor arithmetic or poor assumptions or, at the other extreme, may reflect the desire to make the state or the program look good.

The point of these examples is not to suggest that one or another of the states or systems is attempting to mislead or misstate; rather, it is to demonstrate the extreme variability in what the different states report, if at all, and how they go about doing it. The point is to highlight the importance of and need for reliable and consistent information that can enlighten discussion about school volunteers and to emphasize that such information is not available at the present time, either at the national level or the state or local level. Finally, these examples serve once again to remind the Congress and those in the executive branch charged with determining the state of education and providing guidance and support that they cannot depend currently on state-derived and state-developed information to assist and guide them in their tasks. Unfortunately, as we have seen, all too often the data fall far short of the task.

EDUCATION PARTNERSHIPS

In recent years, the roles of business and industry in the education process have changed markedly. Certainly, business and industry have always had and shown interest in the schools and, especially, in the type of graduates they produced. However, as long as the labor market supply was adequate or in excess, interest was not one of concern nor was it expressed in any major form of contribution to the process. With the recognition that the entry pool of workers is shrinking and that new recruits are not only more difficult to find but also less well trained than might be desired, the focus of attention by industry and business has shifted to one of overt participation in education, in hopes of meeting their needs. This changed participation led to what are now known as education partnerships, which have taken many forms, ranging from the provision by business and industry of money and equipment to providing different types of expertise to assist in and further the education process. Since this form of activity seemed to be growing rapidly, during the 1987–1988 academic year NCES undertook to measure both the size of the phenomenon and the change since an earlier survey (1983–1984).

The most recent study showed that there were an estimated 140,800 education partnerships between public schools and outside sponsors as of the 1987–1988 academic year (National Center for Education Statistics, 1989). The most frequent sponsors of education partnerships were businesses and civic organizations or service clubs. Forty percent of all public schools participated in partnerships, and 24 percent of all public school students were reported directly in them. These schools averaged 4.6 partnerships each. These numbers represent a substantial increase from the earlier survey in 1983–1984, when there were approximately 40,400 partnerships in existence and an estimated 17 percent participation among public schools.

Partnerships were particularly prevalent in the southeastern region of the country, where some 54 percent of public schools reported participation in an education partnership; in other regions, participation ranged from 32 to 39 percent. Overall, just under one-half (46 percent) of the secondary schools had education partnerships, as compared with one-third of the elementary schools. School participation in partnerships was directly related to school size, ranging from 30 percent in small schools to 57 percent in large schools. Finally, poverty appeared to be a key determinant in the presence of a partnership program in a school, with the number rising for schools with larger poverty student bodies.

The overriding support received from the partnerships was in the form of goods and services. About three-fourths of the schools reported this type of support, about one-fourth received money contributions, and one-third received a combination of goods, services, and money. The specific services that schools received consisted for the most part of the use of guest speakers from the partnership, the use of sponsors' facilities, and the provision of student incentive programs, such as student scholarships or awards. Of particular note was the finding that principals initiated most partnership arrangements in existence during the 1987–1988 school year. Some 52 percent of all schools were involved in partnerships initiated by a principal, compared with about 25 percent of schools involved because of the efforts of others, such as superintendents, coordinators, or teachers.

RECOMMENDATIONS

About 1 million people were expected to serve as volunteers in the nation's public school systems during the 1987–1988 school year, according to information collected by the NCES. Almost 47,300 schools, or about 60 percent of the nation's elementary and secondary schools, reported the use of volunteers, averaging almost 21 volunteers per school.

These facts about volunteers provide a reasonable framework within which one can begin to understand the contributions and importance of volunteers to the educational process in the nation. In this situation, as in so many others, reliable, consistent, timely, and accurate information becomes the guidepost to where the nation has been, where it is, and where it wishes to go. At present, there is a paucity of such information.

It is the hope of the committee that the recent developments by NCES in obtaining information on volunteers is but a starting point and that our comments, caveats, and recommendations will serve to move the process forward so that policy makers and others concerned with this area can understand and take for granted that "the right thing is being measured and it is being measured right!"

- The committee recommends that the National Center for Education Statistics be given responsibility for the collection, analysis, and publication of national data on the use of volunteers in schools.

- The committee recommends that the National Center for Education Statistics use its existing advisory committees to define both the data content to be collected and the appropriate frequency of collection.

- The committee recommends that the National Center for Education Statistics consult with state and local school officials, with policy makers, and with parties concerned with the use of volunteers in schools to ensure that full cooperation is forthcoming in effecting the collection of useful and usable information.

- The committee further proposes that the U.S. Department of Education provide leadership to the states and, given willingness on their part to participate, provide both technical and limited short-term financial assistance in initiating state-level periodic collections of data on the use of volunteers in the public schools.

REFERENCES

Center for Education Statistics
1986   E.D. Tabs; The 1985 Public School Survey, Early Tabulations. Washington, D.C.: U.S. Department of Education.
Council of Chief State School Officers
1988   Council Policy Statements, 1988. Washington, D.C.: Council of Chief State School Officers.
Hodgkinson, A., and M. Weitzman
1986a   The Charitable Behavior of Americans, Findings from a National Survey. Conducted by Yankelovich, Stally and White, Inc. Washington, D.C.: Independent Sector.
1986b   Dimensions of the Independent Sector, A Statistical Profile. 2d Ed. Washington, D.C.: Independent Sector.
Independent Sector
1986   American Volunteer 1985, An Independent Sector Summary Report. Washington, D.C.: Independent Sector.
National Center for Education Statistics
1989   Education Partnerships in Public Elementary and Secondary Schools. Washington, D.C.: U.S. Department of Education, Office of Educational Research and Improvement. CS-89-060.

4

Review of Research and Evaluation Literature on School Volunteerism

As part of its inquiry into the use of volunteers in schools, the committee conducted a search for literature and research over the past three decades on the subject of school volunteerism. The information bases examined by the committee included the U.S. Department of Education's Educational Resources Information Center (ERIC); the Library of Congress's index of published and unpublished doctoral dissertations and masters' theses; indexes of professional journals and other publications in education, sociology, and psychology; computerized subject-matter indexes provided by the Library of Congress and a number of organizations; and a variety of materials, including annual reports, prepared by volunteer programs and school districts. An annotated bibliography of the literature is included as Appendix B of this report.

The committee also reviewed a number of articles about school volunteers published during the 1970s and 1980s in education periodicals and professional journals, which are included in the annotated bibliography. Manuals published by professional organizations and others to assist school districts in organizing and managing school volunteer programs were also examined by the committee; although not considered part of the research base, these are listed in the annotated bibligraphy. In addition, the committee examined many school volunteer programs that produce brochures, manuals, promotional materials, and annual reports that are not included in the bibliography but that can be obtained from the programs themselves.

This review addresses reported research on school volunteerism only. Many other areas of education research—such as use of paid paraprofessionals, parental involvement, community education, and the growing involvement of business in partnerships with schools—may have a bearing on this study but, because of constraints of time and resources, the committee did not investigate them.

THE RESEARCH

For purposes of this review, the research studies have been grouped into three general divisions: the use of volunteers in instructional support activities, the effects of volunteers on other than the academic achievement of students, and the effects of volunteers on schools and classrooms. Many studies overlap and could be included in more than one of those sections, but each study is referenced only once.

Use of Volunteers in Instructional Support Activities

Tutoring

According to data on volunteer utilization, one of the services most commonly provided by volunteers in schools is tutoring. Tutoring has also been more extensively studied than any other volunteer activity. The committee identified a number of studies dealing specifically with tutoring by volunteers; of these, almost all reported academic gains for tutored students greater than those for students who were not tutored or greater than would otherwise have been expected for the tutored students. In no instance did researchers report negative effects on academic performance. Researchers also saw effects of tutoring other than academic, including increased confidence and self-esteem on the part of students. In the case of peer and cross-age tutoring, both academic and psychological benefits were reported for the tutors as well.

Tutoring is recognized as an effective teaching method. Bloom (1984) found that with a trained tutor 98 percent of students perform better academically than those taught in conventional classrooms with one teacher. Cohen and others (1982), in a meta-analysis of findings from 65 independent evaluations of school tutoring programs that used a variety of staffing patterns, found most of the programs had positive effects on academic performance and attitudes of tutees and positive effects on tutors.

Among the studies of volunteer tutoring was an analysis conducted in 1972 with funding from the U.S. Department of Education. Plantec and others (1972), in a final report on the pilot "Project Upswing," supported by the Office of Education, described programs in four cities—Denver, Colorado; Oxford, Mississippi; St. Louis, Missouri; and San Francisco, California—that tried to determine whether 1st grade children with minimal learning difficulties can be aided by volunteer tutors. In each program, children selected by their teachers were randomly assigned to three equal-sized groups; one group was given trained volunteer tutors, one had untrained volunteer tutors, and a third group was untutored. Plantec reported that tutored children made greater gains in reading than control group children whether tutors had been trained or not, and gains in reading skills were accompanied by gains in self-esteem.

Another federally supported school volunteer project, funded under Title III of the Elementary and Secondary Education Act in the mid-1970s, included an evaluation of the performance in reading and mathematics of students in grades 5–6 in Dade County, Florida, public schools who were assisted by trained parent volunteer tutors, compared with unaided students (Dade County Public Schools, 1975). The study involved 236 students who were 1 or more years below national norms in mathematics and reading achievement. Tutored students made more than 1-year grade equivalent gains in reading, while untutored students gained only one-third year. Results were similar in mathematics.

Eberwein and others (1976), in a selected review of 34 studies on the effects of volunteer tutoring programs in reading, noted that experimental students generally showed greater academic progress with tutors than without. Tutored children made significantly greater gains in reading skills, including word knowledge, composite reading, and reading comprehension, than did untutored students in control groups. Tutoring, in the studies reviewed, was provided by parents, other adult volunteers, and cross-age volunteers.

Peer or cross-age tutors—elementary or secondary students of the same age as the tutees or slightly older—are used in many schools, and Hedin (1987) reports they may be even more effective than adult tutors. In a meta-analysis of tutoring, Cohen and others (1982) found that in 45 of 52 achievement studies, students tutored by other students scored higher on examination performance than students in conventional classes. A study of a "turn-about" program in Florida (Dade County Public Schools, 1980) reported that students in grades 1–6 who were tutored by 7th and 9th grade students made greater gains on standardized tests than untutored students. Gains were even greater for students when tutors received special training.

Hedin noted that tutoring by students "could potentially be a great asset to those faced with having to teach large classes of students with widely divergent ability." Adding scores of "auxiliary teachers" who can provide individual attention to students at no additional cost has significant potential for increasing the teacher's productivity, she said (Hedin, 1987).

College students are also effective volunteer tutors, according to a recent study by the U.S. Department of Education (Reisner, Petry, and

Armitage, 1989). The study, mandated by Congress in the Elementary and Secondary School Improvement Amendments of 1988, reported on tutoring programs for disadvantaged elementary and secondary students that involved college students as tutors. A survey conducted in connection with the study found that volunteer tutoring and mentoring programs are under way in 1,700 of the nation's 3,200 colleges and universities, and most of them designate tutoring as their primary service. Effects on tutored students included improvements in test scores, grades, or academic ability (reported by 11 of 19 projects reviewed); improvement in motivation and attitude toward education; exposure to new environments and role models; and increase in self-esteem.

Other Instructional Support Activities

While tutoring has been the volunteer activity most often studied by researchers, there is also a body of research studies on the use of volunteers in other instructional activities. In the studies reviewed, volunteers participated with teachers in a variety of ways to augment and reinforce learning; in some cases, teachers and volunteers were trained together to implement innovative or experimental instructional strategies. The committee believes that this research suggests promising new directions for school volunteerism.

Among the examples of nontutorial volunteer activities were a San Francisco immigrant literacy project (see Armstrong, Northcutt, and Davis, 1987) in which volunteers read to and listened to reading by students in grades K–5 who had limited English skills. The researchers concluded that a teacher-volunteer team approach can be effective in enhancing students' attitudes toward and enjoyment of reading and can also improve basic language arts skills. They also found that students made much greater gains in grade level when the project was implemented schoolwide for a full academic year than when it was implemented for 6 months in one classroom.

In another San Francisco project (see Armstrong and Crowe, 1987), teachers and volunteers were teamed for the purpose of developing students' problem-solving skills in mathematics. Both teachers and volunteers received training in problem-solving approaches. Students showed 20–25 percent increases in problem-solving ability without loss of computational skills and demonstrated statistically significant increases in positive attitudes toward mathematics.

High school foreign-language students increased their oral proficiency in a target language when teams of teachers and college student volunteers focused on conversational activities rather than grammar and sentence patterns (see Armstrong, Davis, and Northcutt, 1987). The most frequent use of volunteer time was to lead students in conversation.

Use of volunteers to give extra time and attention to handicapped students was given impetus by the Education for All Handicapped Children Act of 1975, which called for "mainstreaming" handicapped children in regular classrooms whenever possible. Cuninggim and Mulligan (1979) cited examples of programs in which volunteers aided in developing academic skills and self-confidence in mildly handicapped students. Schulze (1979) found that given proper training and supervision, volunteers helped dyslexic students achieve significant academic gains. In another project, a tutorial relationship between high school volunteers and peer-aged moderately retarded students participating in individually prescribed programs of physical activity produced significant improvement in gross motor abilities in the students (Bechtold, 1977).

In a report published by the National Center for Research in Vocational Education, Katz (1984) described the benefits of involving volunteers in vocational education; the report includes guidelines for monitoring program progress and evaluating the effects of the program.

Effects on Students Other Than Academic Achievement

Many research projects were looking for, and found, effects other than academic achievement for school volunteer programs. The effects include attitudinal changes in students, measured in terms of classroom behavior, attendance, or staying in school, rather than on academic outcomes. Much of the evidence from this type of research is perceptual: teachers and volunteers are asked how they feel about or perceive certain activities. However, data on school or class attendance as an indication of change are also often analyzed as part of the study. The approaches used to obtain these kinds of data included questionnaires completed by teachers, school administrators, and volunteers. This research bears out anecdotal reports that students grow in self-esteem and confidence as the result of interactions with volunteers.

For example, teachers and volunteers who completed a detailed questionnaire about their perceptions of a Florida school volunteer program (Schaffner, 1987) said that the presence of volunteers in classrooms affected student learning and attitudes positively, as evidenced by improvement in behavior and attitudes as well as test scores. Carney and others (1987), using the Piers-Harris Children's Self-Concept Scale to measure attitudinal changes in children in a "grandparent" program in grades 3–5, reported significant increases in self-concept scores for students in grade 3, though not in grades 4 and 5, as the result of the grandparent program. Qualitative information from teachers indicated they believed children's self-concept had improved. In another program, the Federal City Council, a civic organization in Washington, D.C., recruited scientists and mathematicians to serve as volunteers in D.C. public schools in 1986–1987. After a year in which these volunteers went into schools to lecture, conduct demonstrations, coach students for competitions, and lead science and math clubs, students were asked if their feelings about science and math had changed. Students reported they were more likely to study science and math and to seek science- and math-related careers as a result of the volunteers' interest and encouragement (Federal City Council, 1987). Many of the studies on tutoring cited above also studied and reported on positive changes in attitudes and behavior of students as a result of their work with volunteers.

Effects of Volunteers on Schools and Classrooms

Apart from the effects of volunteer interventions on students, research indicates that volunteer involvement positively affects the structure and operation of classrooms, the teaching practices of teachers, and public attitudes toward education.

One of the most important studies in this area was conducted by Hedges (1972) in Canada. Hedges created a model for volunteer parent involvement and evaluated volunteer use in three schools that implemented the model. In one case, the scheduled presence of volunteers freed teachers to engage in curriculum development; in another, volunteers enabled the school to mainstream handicapped students; and in the third school, large numbers of volunteers in a classroom allowed the teacher to individualize instruction and to give more time to "higher-order" functions such as initiating and evaluating learning. Students in the third school made dramatic gains in comparison with the control classes in all of the measured objectives, with an average gain in reading comprehension of 2.0 years. Although evaluation by the developer of a program must be interpreted with caution, the committee was interested in the Hedges study as a promising avenue for further research.

Streit (1975) examined the effect of an instructional volunteer program on an elementary school in Michigan. Students taught reading skills by volunteers made progress, and there were positive changes in attitude, social adjustment, overall academic achievement, and letter grades. Teacher effectiveness was greater because of volunteers, but some teachers viewed volunteers as a threat. Parents whose children worked with an instructional volunteer supported the program, and volunteers expressed more understanding of school problems than they had previously.

A 3-year evaluation (Armstrong and Crowe, 1987) of a program in which student volunteers from colleges of teacher education worked with teachers in grades 2–5 to improve students' math skills through cooperative learning and use of manipulatives found that students maintained and in some cases increased computation skills in spite of the shift away from drill and practice classroom teaching strategies. Teachers reported that having a trained volunteer in the classroom was one of the most valuable aspects of the project, and the presence of the volunteer was identified as the critical ingredient in implementing cooperative learning.

A survey of Maryland school principals (Vassil, Harris, and Fandetti, 1988) found that principals believe school programs have been positively affected by volunteer services, including an increase in resources for instructional programs, improvement in students' behavior, and more use of school facilities after regular school hours. Principals also noted that volunteer services help to forge closer links between schools and community agencies and business and industry. Holzmiller (1982) used regression methodology to determine the effects of volunteer aides on classrooms of children in grades 2–5. He found that volunteers enhanced teacher effectiveness and increased student achievement in reading and grammar on all grade levels, irrespective of aptitude, sex, and ethnicity.

Hill (1980) was apparently the first to attempt a research analysis of the structure of volunteer programs themselves. She classified characteristics of 20 award-winning volunteer programs by frequency, producing a checklist of elements that are characteristic of successful programs. Organization and management were key factors. She suggested development of a workable model for recording and analyzing the volunteer contributions to show cost-benefit ratios and a method for collecting data from the client—the student.

The committee is aware that volunteers provide noninstructional services to schools that may significantly affect daily operations. This kind of volunteer activity—working in school offices and libraries, supervising playgounds and cafeterias, monitoring field trips, fund raising, and coaching, for example—has not been the subject of research, so far as the committee could find, but data on school volunteerism suggest that it accounts for many thousands of volunteer hours each year.

The Problem of Evaluation in Volunteer Programs

In its review of research and from other observations, the committee became aware that evaluation of student or program outcomes is a problem for school volunteer programs. To some extent this is understandable: good evaluation is expensive, and few local school systems have the staff or resources to conduct it. It is usually difficult to justify evaluation expenditures for a "free" or "low-cost" activity such as a volunteer program.

Research into the effects of volunteers on student academic achievement is often complicated because of mixed program objectives. For example, when volunteers have been welcomed into schools, it has often been for reasons (including public relations or parent involvement) that are not directly related to their effectiveness in aiding students or their contribution to the educational objectives of the schools. Identifying and measuring their impact on students under these conditions is particularly difficult. When the primary objective is public relations or parent involvement, these aspects of volunteer programs have not seemed to require examination. Furthermore, educators are generally reluctant to ascribe educational change to any one factor, pointing out that many influences on students occur at the same time, including, for example, improved curriculum, skillful teaching, or parental support. It is therefore often difficult to identify and measure the contribution of volunteer intervention to academic improvement.

These and other factors currently inhibit rigorous evaluation of the effects of volunteer programs. In summary:

- Volunteer programs usually work on small budgets, and good evaluation is expensive. Few school administrators or volunteer coordinators have been willing to divert resources from service to evaluation.
- Evaluation is a demanding craft. Not many people are well trained in its exercise.
- It has generally been taken for granted that volunteers help students. Very few people raised the question of how much benefit was being provided. It did not seem an important issue to quantify the gains from a "free resource."
- Student achievement is not always the best measure of volunteer effectiveness. Aside from the long-standing debate about the appropriateness of test scores as a measure of educational progress, volunteer programs can question the use of test scores to measure their effectiveness on several grounds:

    —Not all volunteers work in classrooms with children. Some do clerical work to relieve the teacher of paperwork, some take children on trips, some work in the school library on such tasks as cataloging and ordering. Some prepare exhibits and displays. It is inappropriate to judge such contributions on the basis of gains in student achievement.

    —Even in the classroom, some of what volunteers offer is a wider view of the world: they tell stories about local history; they offer windows on a wide range of careers; they are available to listen to children and hear their views and concerns. Again, gains on achievement tests are not appropriate assessments of such activities.

—When volunteers do provide instruction, they are not the only people who are teaching the children. The teacher or teachers of the school are simultaneously involved in instruction. Methodologically, there is a major problem: How is it possible to single out the unique contribution that volunteers make to children's test scores? This question is particularly difficult since volunteers do not work with a random sample of students, but usually with students most in need of extra help.

Despite these limitations, the committee concluded that information from evaluations, when properly conducted, is likely to result in significant improvements in the use of volunteers in education. The committee therefore urges and supports evaluation, under the following conditions:

1. Student gains on achievement tests are not the only, or necessarily the best, outcome measure to use. Since volunteer programs encompass a broad range of goals, evaluation should consider the outcomes relevant to each program in its own setting.

2. Multiple measures of outcomes should be used.

3. Evaluations should look not only at outcomes but also at the process of the program under study. That is, evaluation should study the specific activities that volunteers undertake, the frequency with which they are performed, and the conditions under which they occur. Most important of all, the process (activities) by which the program is implemented should be related to the outcomes achieved. In that way, evaluation begins to specify the concrete kinds of activities that are more, or less, successful in achieving different kinds of outcomes. Then, evaluations can do more than render judgment on a program: they can show which kinds of activities are more effective in achieving specific ends, and they can point the way to improvement in program design and implementation.

4. Qualititative methods for collection and analysis of evaluation data can be just as useful as quantitative methods. The choice of evaluation data and methods depends on the specific intent and focus of a particular study. There is now sufficient evidence that volunteers have positive effects on students: what is needed is more sophisticated information on how volunteers affect students and how to optimize the positive effects.

In light of the difficulties of designing and conducting adequate evaluation, and its cost, the committee believes that federal and state governments and private foundations should support studies that will provide guidelines to program administrators and educators on appropriate means of evaluating the effects of volunteers in schools.

SUMMARY AND RECOMMENDATIONS

The committee was impressed that findings about the effects of school volunteers in the reported research were almost uniformly positive. Conversely, almost nothing indicated negative effects resulting from volunteer use in the schools. We point out, however, that the bulk of the studies relate to tutoring. In this area, the reasonably large number of rigorous studies conducted over the past two decades persuade us of the positive academic results of volunteer activities. Many of these studies also obtained and reported on noncognitive gains, including improvements in motivation and attitudes toward education, exposure to new environments and role models, and increase in self-esteem.

Nevertheless, it is also necessary to point out that the body of research on school volunteers, except for studies of tutoring, is limited in quantity and scope. Most of the studies are local and often involve only a few classes or a small number of students. A number of those reviewed were poorly conceived, with apparent faults in methodology, so that their results were inconclusive. For example, a number of the researchers noted that the time allotted for their investigations was too short to measure change and that outcomes such as reading improvement might have been different if the volunteer interventions had continued for longer periods. Some of these investigations were experiments set up to test specific research hypotheses with respect to use of volunteers in the classroom. Often these experiments were conducted in schools that had no previous use of volunteers and that had to deal with the shakedown process inevitable when something new is added to the instructional delivery system. In some instances there were only a few studies on which to base conclusions. The importance of training on volunteer effectiveness, for example, rests on only a few studies that attempted to examine this variable and other studies that imply but do not measure its importance. The committee is persuaded that for some activities, particularly for effective tutoring and mentoring, training is an important factor, but more and better conceived studies on this variable are clearly needed.

More broadly, the committee became aware of a number of issues or questions on which research is needed, particularly if use of volunteers in schools is expanded. For example, the question of equity needs further research. Because use of volunteers is largely determined at the individual school level, it is possible that some schools in well-to-do areas, possibly those with well-informed or knowledgeable parents, are more likely to use volunteers than schools in poorer areas. If so, how expanded use of volunteers could be implemented so that it does not increase inequity between schools is a question for research.

The cost of volunteer programs is another topic that needs study. Because it is assumed that school volunteers are a low-cost, even free resource, little attention has been paid to the "cost-benefit ratio" of volunteer programs. Generally, it is assumed that the value of volunteer services far exceeds the administrative and other costs associated with such programs. However, available studies addressing this question are oversimplified, and we urge further research and analysis in this area.

With increasing use of computers and telecommunications in education, the question of the role that volunteers might play in enhancing use of technology by students should also be investigated. Furthermore, as already indicated, there has been virtually no research on the considerable use of volunteers in clerical and other supportive activities. Anecdotal evidence attests to the value of such services, but research and analysis are needed to provide us with a better understanding of the impact of such services.

Studies of the effects of volunteers on the structure and operation of schools and classrooms, the practices of teachers, and public attitudes are also needed. The studies now available provided the committee with some insights, but much more needs to be known. Finally, more research and evaluation focused directly on the impact of volunteers are needed. Studies now available to us on attitudes, behavior, and other effects are largely based on teacher or volunteer perceptions; rarely is information obtained directly from the student. In summary, the committee concludes that additional research and evaluation studies on the use of volunteers in schools are needed.

- **The committee recommends that the federal government and foundations provide funding for some systematic analysis and evaluation of the content, implementation, and impact of school volunteer programs.**

- **The committee recommends that the U.S. Department of Education and private foundations and universities sponsor specific investigations and examinations of the role volunteers play in implementing education practices found to be effective in improving student learning.**

REFERENCES

Armstrong, Patricia M., and Amy Bassell Crowe
1987 Final Evaluation Report, Project Math in Action. San Francisco School Volunteers, San Francisco Unified School District.

Armstrong, Patricia M., Patrick Davis, and Cherise Northcutt
1987 Final Evaluation Report, Project Year 1986-87, Project Interconnections II. San Francisco School Volunteers, San Francisco Unified School District.

Armstrong, Patricia M., Cherise Northcutt, and Patrick Davis
  1987 Year End Evaluation Reports, Project Years 1985–86 and 1986–87, Project Book
        Your Time. San Francisco School Volunteers, San Francisco Unified School District.

Bechtold, Warren Willard
  1977 The Effect of a Tutorial Relationship Between High School Student Volunteers
        and Peer-Aged Moderately Retarded Students Participating in Individually Pre-
        scribed Programs of Physical Activity. Unpublished doctoral dissertation. School
        of Education, Boston University.

Bloom, B. S.
  1984 The search for methods of group instruction as effective as one-to-one tutoring.
        Educational Leadership (May):4–17.

Carney, John M., Judith E. Dobson, and Russell L. Dobson
  1987 Using senior citizen volunteers in the schools. *Journal of Humanistic Education
        and Development* (March):136–143.

Cohen, Peter A., James A. Kulik, and Chen-Lin C. Kulik
  1982 Educational outcomes of tutoring: a meta-analysis of findings. *American Educa-
        tional Research Journal* (Summer):237–248.

Cuninggim, Whitty, and Dorothy Mulligan
  1979 *Volunteers and Children with Special Needs.* Alexandria, Va.: National Association
        of Partners in Education.

Dade County Public Schools
  1975 *School Volunteer Development Project.* Miami, Fla.: Dade County Public Schools.

Dade County Public Schools
  1980 *Evaluation of Training for Turnabout Volunteers.* Miami, Fla.: Dade County Public
        Schools.

Eberwein, Lowell, Lois Hirst, and Susan Magedanz
  1976 An Annotated Bibliography on Volunteer Tutoring Programs. Paper presented
        at annual meeting of Southeast Regional Reading Conference. University of
        Kentucky.

Federal City Council
  1987 Scientists in the Classroom: One School District's Experience with Science and
        Mathematics Volunteers in Elementary and Secondary Schools. Washington,
        D.C.: Federal City Council.

Hedges, Henry G.
  1972 Using Volunteers in Schools: Final Report. Ontario Department of Education,
        Ontario Institute for Studies in Education, St. Catherines Niagara Center, Toronto,
        Canada.

Hedin, Diane
  1987 Students as teachers: a tool for improving school climate and productivity.
        Social Policy (Winter):42–47.

Hill, Corrine Paxman
  1980 A Comparative Study of Formal Volunteer Programs in Educational Settings.
        Unpublished doctoral dissertation. Department of Educational Administration,
        University of Utah.

Holzmiller, Robert Joseph
  1982 Using Volunteer Aides in a K–5 Elementary School. Unpublished doctoral dis-
        sertation. University of Arizona.

Katz, Douglas S.
  1984 *Volunteers and Voc Ed. Information Series 271.* Columbus, Ohio: National Center
        for Research in Vocational Education, Ohio State University.

Plantec, Peter M., B. Paramore, and J. Hospodar
  1972   *Final Report on the Evaluation of Project Upswing's First Year.* Silver Spring, Md.: Operations Research, Inc.
Reisner, Elizabeth R., Christene A. Petry, and Michele Armitage
  1989   A Review of Programs Involving College Students as Tutors or Mentors in Grades K–12. Prepared for the U.S. Department of Education. Policy Studies Associates, Inc., Washington, D.C.
Schaffner, Deanne
  1987   A Study of the Effectiveness of Volunteers in the Classroom. Unpublished master's thesis. College of Education, University of Central Florida.
Schulze, Sally Reddig
  1979   Evaluation of a Paraprofessional/Volunteer Program to Improve the Reading, Language, and Math Skills of Dyslexic Students. Unpublished doctoral dissertation. Department of Education, Case Western Reserve University.
Streit, John Frederick
  1975   The Effect of an Instructional Volunteer Program on an Elementary School. Unpublished doctoral dissertation. Wayne State University.
Vassil, Thomas V., Oliver C. Harris, and Donald V. Fandetti
  1988   The Perception of Public School Administrators Regarding Community Education Programs Sponsored by Maryland State Department of Education. Survey commissioned by Adult and Community Education Branch, Division of Instruction, Maryland State Department of Education. University of Maryland School of Social Work and Community Planning, Baltimore, Md.

5

Some Exemplary
Volunteer Programs

Supplementing the analysis of available data and the review of the research literature, committee members and staff made 13 site visits to "exemplary" volunteer programs. The main purpose of the visits, fulfilling a major study objective, was to provide committee members with first-hand exposure to a variety of volunteer programs, to talk with and question those involved in giving and receiving services, and to interact with policy makers and teachers. The visits also resulted in a detailed description of each program based on personal observation, as well as analysis of data and materials on the program. This chapter presents summaries of the committee's observations and findings from the site visits.

Most visits involved teams of two or three members and staff for 1 or 2 days: 1 1/2 days at the site and 1/2 day for reviewing and consolidating notes and other information materials. During the visits, extensive interviews were conducted with the volunteer coordinator or other person responsible for the operation of the program at the city or district level. Interviews were also conducted when possible with the school superintendent and other top administrative or policy officials and at building sites with the principal, teachers, and the school volunteer coordinator. In many instances, interviews were also held with volunteers and students. Interview guides for each of these groups were prepared to help assure that some agreed-on core questions would be asked at all sites. These site visits and interviews could not confer instant expertise, but they did serve to give the committee and staff a feeling for what volunteers actually do, how the different levels of the school system view such programs, and how each of the programs is organized and operated.

Without exception, all of the site visit hosts were extremely cooperative, willingly answering all questions and helping the team see specific instances of exemplary use of volunteers. Although the case histories in this chapter are based on materials supplied at each site as well as notes from interviews and observations, the committee takes responsibility for the descriptions and observations.

Selection of sites was based on programs suggested by state and local coordinators of volunteer services organizations, including the National School Volunteers Program (now the National Association of Partners in Education), the National Education Association, the National PTA, the National School Boards Association, and others.

Recognizing the difficulty of selecting a few programs that are labeled as exemplary, the committee established the following criteria for a program to be selected:

- have administrative- and policy-level support and show evidence of sound organization and management;
- have written goals and objectives, clearly defined, based on school or district priorities and supported by a needs assessment process;
- have a written plan of action (i.e., procedures for administering program design);
- be largely student centered and involve human interaction;
- collect data and information (e.g., the number of volunteers used, number of students served) and conduct periodic evaluations of progress made toward goals and objectives; and
- have been in operation for at least 2 years.

In addition, an effort was made to select programs from different parts of the country and from small and medium-sized as well as large school districts. The committee also attempted to select programs representing a variety of organizational arrangements.

The number of programs visited was limited by the time and funds available. Although the programs reviewed met the criteria established for "exemplary" programs, the committee was very much aware that there are dozens, probably hundreds, of others that are as good or possibly even better. The descriptions of the 13 programs in this chapter (presented in alphabetical order) should be regarded, therefore, as illustrative of some of the many models that have been developed in different parts of this country, largely over the last two decades.

The committee recognized the existence of unsuccessful programs. To deal with this issue, several such programs were identified, and persons were interviewed to provide some insight as to why the programs were unsuccessful. Furthermore, the committee also questioned persons interviewed during site visits about problems they encountered and how they resolved them. We asked questions about what inhibited successful operation—such as what happens when administrators, teachers, or teacher organizations are disinterested or even hostile toward use of volunteers, questions on recruitment problems, adequate screenings, liability issues, commitment problems, and others—that the committee had identified as possible inhibiting or even negative factors. Our findings from the interviews are addressed in the next chapter on factors in school volunteerism.

ANN ARBOR, MICHIGAN

The visit was to the primarily Teaching-Learning Communities (T-LC) program, an intergenerational program housed in the Scarlett Middle School in Ann Arbor. The committee also visited briefly a T-LC program in one elementary school, Carpenter Elementary. In the T-LC program, senior citizens are recruited from the community to work with students. The program emphasizes development of relationships across generations, with the major goal of enhancing the self-esteem of both volunteers and students. The major focus is on working with youths who are at risk of dropping out. A component of the secondary school T-LC program involves college students from the University of Michigan who perform much the same functions as the senior volunteers.

Ann Arbor, home of the University of Michigan, is a medium-sized university town, with traditionally high expectations of its public schools. The community recently approved a $30 million bond issue for education, although 70 percent of the population has no children in school. The district's 14,000 students attend 3 high schools, 5 middle schools, and 22 elementary schools. Overall, the T-LC program operates in 2 middle schools, 2 high schools, and 12 elementary schools in the district—just over one-half of all schools.

An Ann Arbor elementary school art teacher developed the T-LC program almost 20 years ago and is now coordinator of the T-LC program in Ann Arbor secondary schools. Another coordinator has responsibility for the program in elementary schools. The T-LC program is strongly supported by the Ann Arbor Education Association, an affiliate of the National Education Association, which was instrumental in obtaining funding for the program in its early years. The NEA cites the program as a model teacher-created and -supported volunteer activity.

The senior volunteers act in specific roles. As *mentors*, they may talk with students, usually at least once a week, by telephone or in person, helping with concerns about doing well in school or problems with friends or at home. As *career guides*, they visit schools to explain and discuss their careers. As *tutors*, they work with individual children on mastery and practice. As *"grandpersons,"* they go to school, perhaps once a week, to help with creative projects in arts or humanities and their relationship to learning in the areas of basic skills. Because the intergenerational program is based on mutual learning and teaching by volunteers and students, the program is "constantly reinvented," with activities depending on the particular strengths and needs of individual students and volunteers as well as the needs of teachers and administrators in the school. Currently, there are 95 volunteers between the ages of 55 and 94, 60 in elementary schools and 35 in middle schools and high schools; 40 percent are men, and approximately 30 percent are minorities.

The program director explained that it is a fundamental tenet of T-LC that volunteers as well as students learn on the job, so she does little or no training of volunteers beyond a 2-hour orientation. Screening of volunteers for the secondary school program is also minimal; the director says that the program is inclusive rather than exclusive and that she would rarely screen anyone out. However, paid school personnel work closely with volunteers so that liability issues are covered and the volunteer has support when needed.

The principal of Scarlett Intermediate was supportive of the T-LC program. He indicated that in his building the coordinator has responsibility for the program, including record-keeping on volunteers and assignments. At the district level, the superintendent and assistant superintendent for community relationships expressed approval of the T-LC program. They also explained that Ann Arbor has volunteer facilitators or coordinators in other areas such as tutoring in the high schools and a Partners for Excellence Program with local businesses, separate from the T-LC program. The teachers' union supports volunteer programs, and teachers welcome the extra help, they said.

For the program as a whole, evaluations have been conducted since 1975; generally, these are opinion forms that are filled out by students, teachers, principals, and volunteers, with responses scaled from 1 ("definitely yes") to 5 ("definitely no"). These evaluations are overwhelmingly positive about the program. In addition, the college students in the secondary schools, but not the senior volunteers, are evaluated by teachers. In 1987, data collection began on grades, test scores, and attendance.

The committee found a great deal of commitment and caring among volunteers in the T-LC program, and teachers and volunteers were uniformly positive about the program.

BOSTON, MASSACHUSETTS

Boston Partners in Education (BPIE), known as School Volunteers for Boston before 1988, is an independent, apolitical, multicultural organization with the mission of strengthening the education experience of the city's public school students. Serving a school system with a large population of students scoring much lower than the national medians for reading and math on national standardized educational tests, this volunteer service organization works with the school system in a broad array of activities.

The 118 Boston public schools serve approximately 58,600 students: 48 percent are black, 18 percent Hispanic, 8 percent Asian, and 26 percent white. Analysis of Metropolitan Achievement Tests (MAT) scores showed that close to one-half of all Boston public school students need remediation and probably have difficulty understanding their textbooks. As in other cities, most of these students are black and Hispanic; much of the effort of BPIE is directed to working with these youngsters.

The initial operation in 1966 consisted of 28 volunteers in six Boston schools and has grown every year. By 1968 the number was 450; by 1975 it was over 2,000; by 1988 the number was nearly 4,200 persons.

The Boston school volunteer effort was established in 1966 with a Ford Foundation grant to the Public Education Association. Having pioneered a small but promising school volunteer program in New York City schools in 1956, the PEA proposed in 1964 to become a national organization, developing similar progress in the 20 largest cities, including Boston. The grant specified that funding was for the purpose of establishing a national office, including field workers who would identify individuals or agencies in cities willing to design and find funds for a program suited to the particular city. The Council for Public Schools, which already sponsored educational projects in Boston, expressed interest in initiating a school volunteer program with the help of the newly formed National School Volunteer Program and worked out a plan with the Boston School Department. This agreement stipulated that if volunteers were to be permitted in the schools it would have to be under the auspices of a capable and responsible agency that would provide adequate training. Moreover, before placement of any volunteer, a request would have to be made from a particular school. This practice became and still is the program's policy.

From the beginning the decision was made to operate the school volunteers unit in Boston as a nonprofit organization working with the schools. The organization had to raise funds for operating expenses from private foundations and business sources, and it involved the business community from the start. Early recruitment efforts enlisted organizations with a history of volunteer activity, including Junior League, Radcliff Alumnae Association, B'nai Brith, and others. The volunteers themselves were mainly middle-aged, well-educated, and concerned women. Their efforts were so well received by the formerly skeptical teachers that demands for more help increased each year. As the program expanded, we were told it continued to attract middle-income-level women, suburban housewives with former roots in the city, and then men and women with social concerns willing to donate their time. Appeals to the business community resulted in cooperation from a number of corporations, which allowed employees a few hours a week for volunteer work. Another major source tapped was the large college population in the greater Boston area.

By 1972 the organization sought independence from the Council for Public Schools and became the School Volunteers for Boston. In 1988 pursuing a broader mandate, the organization, still operating as a nonprofit organization with a board of directors, changed its name to Boston Partners in Education. Although placement of volunteers in schools remains the major emphasis, BPIE has expanded its goals and activities. Now included are social intervention services, such as a family support network that provides training and information services for families, as well as linkage of families with schools and other community service providers. BPIE also uses staff experts to provide management, consulting, and training services to educators, businesses, and community organizations.

Now one of the largest of the big-city volunteer organizations in the nation, BPIE operates with a budget of over $800,000 and a staff of 25 full- and part-time professionals and 10 consultants. About 25 percent of the funds come from the Boston Public Schools under a contract that includes state funds to aid in the desegregation process; about 60 percent of the funds are from foundations and businesses; and 15 percent come from individual contribution or fee-for-service activities.

One of the most active BPIE programs, in which large numbers of volunteers are involved, comes under the heading of enrichment. More than 1,100 people in the 1987–1988 school year enhanced the curriculum with music, art, peace and justice issues, black history, colonial history, law-related education, alcohol and drug awareness, multicultural studies, and science. Intergenerational programs were another large activity: more than 1,100 volunteers participated in interview, oral history, advocacy, and other programs both in schools and in senior citizen centers, nursing homes, and other facilities for older adults.

Tutoring of reading, math, English as a second language, writing, and computer use was another extensive area of activity. About 642 persons gave weekly tutoring assistance under the direction of teachers in regular and special education classes. Mentoring activities from 347 business volunteers helped students achieve better grades, improve attendance, and plan for higher education. Another 25 persons served as listener/mentors supporting potentially at-risk students through one-on-one sessions. Reading aloud was a supporting activity for 256 volunteers working with elementary school children. Another 230 volunteers gave presentations on their careers, trying to motivate students to stay in school and to set career goals. Volunteers also helped as classroom assistants, supporting individual teachers, and helped school libraries set up creative learning centers. Still others participated as office interns, advisory group members, clerical and field-trip assistants, and helpers in the arts, sciences, social studies, and foreign languages. A small number of university students "adopted" elementary school pupils and shared after-school activities.

Working with each school to determine the needs of individual teachers, BPIE serves as a centralized volunteer recruitment, screening, and placement agency to help meet those needs. Recruitment efforts involve media cooperation, extensive contacts with organizations and businesses, as well as helping each school to involve parents and others in the school community. BPIE also screens new volunteers for the schools, including review of applications, reference checks with police for possible criminal records for all volunteers who may be working in an unsupervised situation with children, assurance that required tuberculin tests are on file, and matching the skills and desires of the volunteers with the stated needs of teachers in each school. Orientation of volunteers, including administrative procedures and what is expected, is conducted each week and as needed. Specialized training for activities such as tutoring for English as a second language and mentoring is provided for the volunteers and the teachers. BPIE also works with the schools to provide recognition for volunteers.

Attempts to experiment with more comprehensive education planning that includes the use of volunteers is under way. In 1988, 39 schools interested in cooperating were selected to participate in this planning effort. Teams from BPIE met with school administrators and teachers to develop plans and procedures for tapping community (including business) resources. This process will be extended to other groups of interested schools in 1989. The planning process, especially the training provided, is considered essential to providing well-coordinated education programs and to the effective use of volunteers in schools.

The independent nonprofit form of BPIE allows the organization considerable freedom to develop linkages with parent, church, religious, and social welfare organizations and other groups concerned with children and youth. Collaboration efforts have resulted in after-school and summer programs and allowed experimentation with providing services such as after-school study halls in church buildings, using business and community volunteers to tutor, help, or simply listen to young people. The independent form of organization also allows considerable freedom in fund raising from foundations and the business community to develop models and experiment with innovative approaches to using volunteers and other services to enhance the education of students in Boston's schools.

BPIE has strong support from the superintendent of schools: charged with a mandate to promote collaboration among the schools, the community, and business, BPIE is a welcome partner in carrying out this mandate. The goals of BPIE are consistent with those of the school board, and the close working relationships and additional resources that BPIE provides are appreciated. The superintendent told the committee that having the BPIE as a collaborator but outside the school system has allowed continuity despite frequent changes in school superintendents and has allowed the program more flexibility and long-term consistency.

Evaluation of BPIE activities, like those of other volunteer efforts, is the weakest part of the program. The organization does do a self-assessment on a regular basis, reviewing its progress toward goals, but this is basically a process review. Teachers and volunteers are required to fill out forms reporting their perceptions of accomplishments, and these are used to pinpoint trouble spots and otherwise manage the program. However, little evaluation of outcomes is attempted. The executive director of the organization told us that some experimental attempts at measuring outcomes will be tried this year, but she pointed to high cost as a major factor inhibiting formal evaluation studies.

CHICAGO, ILLINOIS

Chicago public schools have 400,000 students, a staff of 40,000, and an annual operating budget approaching $2 billion. Total enrollment in the city's 495 elementary schools and 65 high schools has declined by 15 percent since 1978. Approximately two-thirds of the city's students are black; 14 percent are white; and the remainder are Hispanic, Asian, and Native American. Hispanic enrollment has increased by 27 percent since 1978. Slightly more than half of the system's teachers are black.

Under a 1984 consent decree, Chicago has been allowed to use magnet schools as a means of desegregation. Many schools, particularly in the city's concentrated public housing areas, remain all black, and others are largely Hispanic. Our visits included an elementary foreign languages magnet school in which the student population is one-third black, one-third white, and one-third Hispanic, and a neighborhood elementary school in the city's largest housing project, where all of the students are black and most are eligible for federally subsidized free school lunches and breakfasts.

The organized school volunteer program in Chicago dates back to 1982, when the Chicago Community Trust was asked by the superintendent to support the schools at a time of resource cuts. A pilot program called the Chicago Education Corps was developed and was instituted in three subdistricts in 1983, with 300 volunteers in the first semester. In the 1984–1985 school year, the volunteer program became citywide and was given the status of a bureau in the school system. In 1987–1988, the Bureau of Volunteer Programs counted close to 12,000 volunteers in its programs, more than 95 percent of them in the largest program, the Schoolhouse Volunteers.

Principals are asked to send the Bureau of Volunteer Programs a completed and signed application for each volunteer. The bureau aggregates these reports, and prior to an annual citywide recognition ceremony the principal is asked to verify and update a computer printout of all volunteers in the school. Because volunteer programs are administered by one division of the Chicago school system, while Adopt-a-School and the career education program are administered by other divisions, it is hard to compare the numbers reported by the bureau with figures from school systems in which all programs involving volunteers are administered by one office.

The committee spent one day in discussion with the director of the Bureau of Volunteer Programs and her assistant at Chicago public schools headquarters. They showed a video describing the Schoolhouse Volunteers program, explained their strategies for recruiting volunteers, and provided samples of materials that are provided to schools, including a manual for volunteers and a manual for building teams that coordinate the work of volunteers. We also met two assistant superintendents and the associate superintendent for human resources. All expressed support for the district's volunteer program.

As the Chicago program is structured, the director and her two-person staff are responsible for recruiting volunteers citywide, using public service announcements on radio and television, usually contributed by local broadcasters, and posters and flyers prepared by the district's graphics department. At the end of the school year, the Bureau of Volunteer Programs sponsors a districtwide gala to recognize and honor volunteers who have worked during the year.

Day-by-day management of volunteers in school buildings is the responsibility of building teams, usually consisting of the principal or an assistant principal, a teacher (often a resource teacher), and a parent or community volunteer. Any one of the three may serve as the building coordinator. The school recruits its own volunteers, and the building team is expected to train the volunteers, provide orientation to teachers on effective use of volunteers, and keep records of the hours that volunteers work.

Given the size of the Chicago school district and the limited staff of the Bureau of Volunteer Programs, the bureau relies on written materials, including application forms and training manuals, to provide guidance to school teams. On-site technical assistance is available on request. The Bureau of Volunteer Programs oversees five programs in addition to Schoolhouse Volunteers: Homework Hotline, Saturday Scholars, Intergenerational Tutoring, Treasure Hunters, and Lawmakers for Students.

Schoolhouse Volunteers is the basic and largest Chicago volunteer program, in which individuals work in schools as audiovisual aides, library assistants, bilingual aides, classroom assistants, tutors, administrative staff helpers, and community fund raisers. Parents make up almost 80 percent of the Schoolhouse Volunteers program. Others are senior citizens, college students, or anyone with a desire to share expertise and time by helping young people. The bureau reported 11,263 volunteers active in this program in schools during the 1987–1988 school year. Schoolhouse Volunteers are generally recruited by the school in which they will work, through messages sent home to parents, for example. The Bureau of Volunteer Programs does not maintain a bank of potential volunteers, but refers callers to schools in their neighborhoods.

Homework Hotline, a partnership between the Chicago Public Schools and the *Sun-Times* newspaper, is staffed by volunteers from 5 p.m. to 8 p.m., Mondays through Thursdays. Working from offices in the *Sun-Times* building, volunteers answer students' telephone questions about homework on all subjects; the majority of calls concern language arts and mathematics. Volunteers include working and retired teachers, other professionals with academic expertise, and volunteers from businesses in the downtown area who come in after work before going home for the evening. In-service training is provided for all volunteers, and they are familiarized with the systemwide learning objectives of the Chicago public schools. Approximately 80 volunteers staffed the Homework Hotline in 1987–1988. Since the program began, volunteers have fielded more than 25,000 questions.

Saturday Scholars is a program in which sailors from the Great Lakes Naval Base volunteer as tutors for students in grades 4–6 who are identified by their teachers as needing help. Sailors are transported by the school system to selected schools for five consecutive 2-hour Saturday morning sessions, followed by a sixth Saturday at the naval base that features an awards ceremony, a tour of the base, and lunch. Teaching materials and tutoring formats are supplied by the volunteer program, and the sailors receive orientation and training. The Service School Command at the Great Lakes Naval Base provides registration forms for sailors interested in volunteering. Three Saturday Scholars sessions are scheduled during each school year, and registration is limited to 100 students per school. Approximately 1,500 tutors and 1,500 students have been involved in the program.

Intergenerational Tutoring is a collaboration between the Chicago public schools and the city's Department of Aging. Tutoring sessions in which retirees work with students in grades 4–6 are held on Saturdays from

10 a.m. to noon throughout the school year at a facility for the elderly. The Bureau of Volunteer Programs provides in-service training for the volunteers, and students are pretested to determine placement for reading and math tutoring and homework assistance. The program involves approximately 20 tutors and 60 students.

Treasure Hunters is a partnership between Chicago public schools and the Chicago Public Library, intended to enhance reading comprehension and vocabulary for students in grades 4-6 during the summer. Students are recruited from elementary schools near two libraries and tested in vocabulary and comprehension prior to the beginning of the program. Tutoring sessions are then designed to meet their individual needs. Additionally, time is set aside for recreational reading. All students are required to have library cards and are encouraged to participate in other library programs. Volunteers are asked to contribute 3 hours per week; tutoring sessions are held in selected public libraries, and, whenever possible, students are tutored one to one. Approximately 115 volunteers and students are involved at two library sites.

Lawmakers for Students is a series of lectures for 8th grade students. The Bureau of Volunteer Programs has asked each of the 50 Chicago aldermen to volunteer as a lecturer in an elementary school in his or her ward for 5 weeks, on the topics: "Why I Chose to Be an Alderman," "The Structure of the City Council," "Committees I Serve on and What They Do," "My Hopes and Dreams for the City of Chicago," and a fifth topic requested by the students. This series is an extra activity for students; students who participate are expected to complete all regular class assignments. The legislators are believed to serve as role models for the students.

As a form of program evaluation, the Bureau of Volunteer Programs requests that each principal complete a form at the end of the school year indicating the kind of services that volunteers performed in the school, what was best about the program, and whether volunteers helped to make the school better. Volunteers are asked to complete a similar form, with the added question: "What would you like to change about the program?"

The bureau's director also indicated that she has accumulated quantitative data in the form of pre- and posttest results, largely from the Saturday Scholars tutoring programs, that could be analyzed to determine academic gains made by students as the result of volunteer interventions. She said the Bureau of Volunteer Programs lacks the resources to have the data organized and interpreted.

The Chicago public schools are scheduled to be drastically restructured. A recent state law abolished the old Board of Education and regional offices, and each school will be governed by a board made up of parents and community representatives. How the change to school-based management will affect the district's volunteer program is unknown.

The committee visited two elementary schools in Chicago. In both schools, the principal was an active and enthusiastic guide to the volunteer program and clearly was in direct contact with volunteers.

A morning at LaSalle Academy, a language arts magnet school in Chicago's historic Old Town Triangle district on the mid-north side, began with students arriving by bus and car from around the city; Chicago provides transportation to all students who want to attend magnet schools. LaSalle Academy offers instruction in four languages—French, German, Italian, and Spanish—in addition to the regular curriculum. The multilingual approach is clearly apparent in student work posted in the halls. Parents were very visible in the building, performing volunteer activities ranging from leading Junior Great Books sessions to counting lunch money in the school cafeteria. Parent volunteers were assisting with a hands-on science curriculum, and others were working with 1st graders who have reading problems. LaSalle has a not-for-profit corporation that provides financial support for the school through fund raising and donations. Members of the PTA are automatically members of Friends of LaSalle, and businesses are encouraged to participate through the Adopt-a-School Program sponsored by the Board of Education. At the time of our visit, the PTA was seeking board approval to install $10,000 worth of new playground equipment donated by the PTA.

The situation was different at Terrell Elementary, located in one of the poorest neighborhoods in the United States, in a high-rise public housing project on Chicago's south side. Here, all of the students live in public housing. On the day of our visit, however, six parents, one of them a father, were aiding groups of students in the same hands-on science project we had viewed at LaSalle. According to school staff, the volunteering has twofold benefits, since the program requires training for the volunteers in the experiments the students do. One volunteer father was aided in this manner to receive his general equivalency diploma (GED), which is equal to a high school diploma. On the day of our visit, a volunteer mother was sorting donated clothing in a storeroom and the principal introduced a paid clerical aide who had started as a parent volunteer. Parents served as monitors on a trip to the Chicago planetarium, in which kindergartners saw "Santa Claus come down from the sky."

Developing parent support in a community such as the Robert Taylor Homes has to be counted as a major accomplishment for the school and the Chicago volunteer program. According to the Bureau of Volunteer Programs director, Chicago is making a special effort to recruit volunteers from historically hard-to-reach populations such as welfare mothers.

"Volunteering is seen as something rich white ladies do," she said. "But we point out that there is a tradition of volunteering in the black community, where families often look out for their neighbors' children."

Adopt-A-School and Partnerships. In Chicago, the Bureau of Volunteer Programs operates separately from other district programs. It is located in the Office of Human Resources, the Adopt-A-School program is located in the Office of the Assistant to the General Superintendent, and the Bureau of Community Resources is located in the Department of Vocational and Technological Education.

The strategy of the Adopt-A-School program is to pair schools with businesses or other organizations in order to address specific student needs. The school-business partnership draws on its combined resources to develop a program uniquely fitted to the needs of students. Although all Adopt-A-School programs work toward the same general goal of enhancing the quality of education, especially in the basic skills, the programs that each partnership develops are as varied as the needs of the student participants. Any organization that wishes to improve the quality of education through the sharing of its knowledge, experience, and resources may participate in the Adopt-A-School program. In the 1987–1988 school year, a total of 188 organizations sponsored 407 programs in 233 Chicago public schools. The 6-year-old program has matched at least one adopter with each high school. Individual programs have involved as many as 3,300 students and as few as 10. The adopters provide a range of services and support to schools from off-campus visits to places of interest to donations of equipment and supplies.

The Bureau of Community Resources began in 1976 as a career education program and remains entirely career oriented. It operates in 126 elementary schools and 10 high schools and currently involves 520 businesses. At the elementary level, business people come into schools to discuss careers with students in grades 6–8, in a structured program that covers 16 "career clusters." At the high school level, businesses and professional organizations sponsor career centers (in law or health, for example), providing money, equipment, human resources, and sometimes jobs for students. An umbrella organization for the program, the Chicago Careers for Youth Foundation, was corecipient with the Chicago Board of Education in 1988 of a presidential citation for excellence in private sector initiatives.

CONTRA COSTA COUNTY, CALIFORNIA

Contra Costa County in California is located east of San Francisco and Oakland. It has a land area of more than 700 square miles and a population of about 735,000, with more than 116,000 public school students in

193 schools in 18 districts. Almost one-third of the county's students are from minority groups.

The volunteer program in the county is unique, serving only children in the county's detention programs. It relates to the county's Office of Education, which provides an educational program for young people who are wards of the court or have encountered problems in the traditional school setting. These programs range from temporary care for youths awaiting a court appearance or court-ordered placement to maximum security institutional programs for young people who need close supervision. The county also operates an open residential institution for neglected and dependent children. Day care and community school classes are held throughout the county for students unable to function in regular school settings. These day care classes, purposely kept small, are held in church buildings or other facilities rented by the county. There is also a minimum security residential facility for delinquent boys located in a rural part of the county.

Responding to the need for someone to listen, to care, and to help youngsters in these detention programs, the Contra Costa County Court Schools PTA was formed in 1983. Its purpose is to provide volunteers to supplement and extend the services provided by the county to students in detention facilities or otherwise under the jurisdiction of the courts. The organization also provides advocacy for the students and support for the teachers in court schools. This program was organized by a small group of persons in cooperation with the county director of detention schools. The organizers all had considerable experience in the direction of PTA activities at both local and state levels. The program is unique not only because of the population it attempts to serve, but also because it was organized and is operated by PTA volunteers. Unlike most PTA activities, volunteers in this effort are, with few exceptions, not parents of the students they have volunteered to serve.

Activities of this PTA volunteer program include recruiting and placing volunteers and assisting with their orientation and training. Funds raised from a variety of sources are used for transporting volunteers to remote sites; paying for GED testing and certificates for youths who qualify; organizing dinners and other recognition efforts to honor volunteers and teachers; and paying for books, tapes, and other special materials needed but not provided for in the county budget. The volunteer organization takes responsibility for coordinating volunteer activities at each site. Recruitment activities include preparing and placing articles in newspapers and appearing before senior citizen associations and other groups to solicit volunteer help. The PTA volunteer organization also reviews applications of volunteers, provides initial screening and some of the orientation required, and places volunteers with teachers who have been previously contacted by the county education office and asked to express their needs.

The program is not large; approximately 50 volunteers were involved in 1988, serving approximately 600 youths (under 18) in 15 locations. Training is handled on an individual basis by the teachers who use the volunteers. Because the volunteers are dealing with students who have been removed from the regular school system, orientation is also provided by corrections personnel. This orientation includes prescriptions for dealing with youths in detention programs: for example, volunteers are instructed that no telephone numbers or addresses can be exchanged; contact is on a first-name basis only; and volunteers cannot do favors for the youths. Rigid rules of what can and cannot be brought into the institution and what the volunteer can and cannot do are prescribed.

What the volunteers actually do, we were told, is largely traditional. They tutor the students in reading, math, and other topics for which assistance is needed. Many of the youths have missed so much school time that they are several grades behind in reading and even further behind in writing and math skills. Volunteers also help prepare students to take GED exams and provide instruction in art, crafts, music, physical education, and other specialty areas for which skills of volunteers can be matched to the needs expressed by teachers. Volunteers also help some students compete in state writing and art contests and provide clerical or classroom support.

In one unlocked facility housing 74 youths, tutoring by 14 volunteers included practical tasks requested by the students—such as how to prepare a resumé and apply for a job, how to fill out forms to apply for apprenticeship training, or how to prepare for job interviews. Only those youths being held for 9 months or more receive volunteer help. In this institution, volunteers and students were carefully paired so that contact was on a one-to-one basis and always with the same person. Contact with a caring adult willing to talk about future jobs, career possibilities, and other subjects of interest and concern to the youth frequently resulted in a bonding that was as helpful as specific tutoring.

Although prescribed in the "Volunteer Program Guide," little formal evaluation of this program has been conducted. Volunteer coordinators and the volunteer organizers do get informal feedback from teachers and from volunteers themselves. We were told that more formal evaluations are planned, but, to date, information is largely anecdotal and by word of mouth. One administrator of an unlocked facility we visited told us that the kids in his institution are street smart. If they did not feel that they were benefiting from contact with volunteers, they would have run them out of the place. He felt that despite lack of formal evaluations, much good is being accomplished, and he would like more volunteer help if it were available.

Inadequate funding, despite the significant efforts of volunteers at fund raising, was a major factor inhibiting greater use of volunteers. For example, the minimum security facility described above is located in an isolated part of the county. Available funds limited transportation to one large van with a capacity of 15, transporting volunteers from a seniors' center once a week. Additional funds for transportation would allow more volunteer help more often to work with the young inmates in this facility.

The need to depend on volunteers to organize and operate the entire program is another major limiting factor. Describing the volunteer organizers as dedicated, energetic, and knowledgeable persons, extremely generous with their time, the director of the detention program expressed the view that someone in a full-time paid position to organize and coordinate the volunteer effort could, with support from the existing volunteer group, considerably expand the program. The small day programs using a room in closed school buildings or church facilities, for example, could benefit greatly from volunteer help. These are located in poorer areas and usually run by a teacher with some help from an aide. To find volunteers willing to work under these less-than-favorable conditions would require considerable effort. Future plans call for recruiting volunteers from local businesses, seniors who live in the area of the day program, or other members of local communities who might be willing to help. With a full-time paid coordinator working with the volunteer organization, such ideas might be implemented.

Praising the PTA volunteer program for its highly useful contributions, the county superintendent of education said that without the efforts of these high-powered service-oriented volunteers, more formal efforts would be needed, for which funding would be difficult to obtain. He expressed his support for the volunteer effort and said he had good feedback from the administrators and teachers who used volunteers. He noted that in the first few years there had been some teacher resistance (particularly high school teachers) to using volunteers in their classrooms but that this is disappearing as the advantages become known. As training of volunteers improves and volunteers themselves, seeing the results of their efforts, become more committed and more dependable, more teachers are welcoming their help.

CORSICANA, TEXAS

Corsicana, Texas, is a town of 26,000 between Dallas and Houston; like its neighbors, Corsicana has economic problems as the result of declines in the oil industry. The Corsicana Independent School District enrolls 4,800 students in one high school, two middle schools, and six elementary schools. Almost two-thirds of the enrollment are black children; about one-third are white. Hispanic students account for less than 0.2 percent of the school population, although many fall into the at-risk category.

Two years ago a group of Corsicana school teachers asked the National Foundation for the Improvement of Education (NFIE), a foundation of the National Education Association, to fund an early intervention project for children at risk of dropping out of Corsicana schools.

With $5,000 in the first year, and a renewal grant of $10,000 a year later, the teachers launched Project Rescue, a program in which teachers themselves "adopted" children and the community was asked to support similar activities. Students to be adopted were referred by teachers. The program identified poor self-esteem, sometimes arising from cultural differences, as a major problem for the students and decided to try a mix of personal attention, outings, meetings with parents, and identification of needed social and medical services as a way of improving students' perceptions of themselves and their likelihood of succeeding in school.

During the first year, teachers made one-on-one commitments to 60 students, but found that when trips or excursions were planned, they were often dealing with brothers, sisters, and friends who wanted to go along. Parent apathy, originally targeted as a major problem, was found to be primarily a matter of language barrier or lack of knowledge; most parents were responsive and eager to help their children.

Now led by a 3rd grade teacher, the program has no staff and relatively no organization, but volunteers keep meticulous budget records and spend much time publicizing their project at community meetings and in the media. Since all activities take place outside of school, no space in the school system has been required; the Corsicana school district has donated supplies and secretarial staff.

Looking to the end of its NFIE funding next year, the project is putting contributions from the community into a fund to support continued operations and is seeking grant assistance from several sources. NFIE funds have been spent primarily to buy private tutoring for youngsters and released time for teachers; postage, stationery, and printing; production of an explanatory video; and travel expenses of key people. Funds are also allocated to meet the physical, medical, cultural, counseling, and educational needs of students.

Among the ways teachers make contact with their "adoptees" during the school day are inquiries about report cards or special notice of birthdays. For some children, a restaurant meal with a friend is the first time the child has ever eaten out. On a trip to the Texas State Fair in Dallas, teachers found that many children had never been to Dallas, 50 miles away.

The committee found Corsicana's Project Rescue to be warm, caring, and inspiring—a quintessential "feel good" program. Although no evaluations have been conducted, it is hard to believe that the close personal contacts between teachers (and principals) and students is not helpful.

As the program has become visible through media coverage, a number of community members have come forward as volunteer mentors, and many businesses have offered in-kind support. "Finally," one businessman said, "we are hearing something good about our schools."

DADE COUNTY, FLORIDA

The Dade County Public School District in Florida, which includes the city of Miami, has experienced explosive growth during the past 5 years. During the Mariel boatlift in 1980, 15,000 Cuban children a month entered the school system, and, currently, more than 400 students a month arrive from Nicaragua and other Central American countries. Fifty percent of the district's 260,000 students are Hispanic.

A $980 million bond issue approved by voters in 1988 is part of a $1.5 billion school construction and renovation plan under which the district will build 49 new schools, adding to 289 regular schools and 8 alternate schools now in the system. With more than 23,000 full-time and 9,000 part-time employees, the school district is the largest employer in the Miami area.

A school volunteer program began in Dade County in the 1970s. Major growth occurred during the 1980s, when the number of volunteers grew to 15,000, including 1,000 business partnerships. There are now volunteer programs in 272 of the county's 289 schools. Dade Partners, a partnership program initiated in 1978, pairs businesses and community organizations with schools in a variety of volunteer activities, and a Corporate Volunteer Program asks employers to give employees 2 hours a week of released time to volunteer in schools.

Several years ago Florida became the first state in the country to enact legislation supporting school volunteerism. School districts receive an annual allocation from the state for volunteer activities; in Dade County, this allocation is approximately $80 per school and helps to pay for a district staff of nine professionals and four clerical employees who are responsible for assisting schools with their volunteer programs. The superintendent of schools in Dade County is very committed to the volunteer program, and volunteer coordinators report directly to a director of community participation.

The principal of each school in the district is asked to select a staff member and a community volunteer to head the school's volunteer program; those leaders are then trained by the district staff to recruit, interview, screen, orient, and place volunteers and to monitor the program. Teachers are expected to provide on-the-job training and to confer regularly with their volunteers.

The district supplies manuals that detail the rights and responsibilities of volunteers and suggest ways for schools to use volunteers productively. Faculty orientation is available to schools on request, to familiarize staff with the objectives, structure, and policies of the school volunteer program; to define in measurable terms the benefits of volunteers; and to eliminate any misconceptions teachers may have. The staff of the Department of Community Participation provides training for volunteers in more than 12 curriculum areas on request, at individual schools or regionally.

The Dade County volunteer program includes a wide array of activities from the standard math and reading tutoring, prekindergarten and kindergarten assistants, and computer assistants to more targeted efforts. *Ambassadors for Public Education* volunteers serve as a communication link between the principal and the community by keeping local businesses and organizations abreast of school activities. *I'm Thumbody* is a program designed to enhance self-esteem in second graders, using a 45-minute film presentation and follow-up activities by a trained volunteer. *Listeners* are volunteers who serve as adult friends, typically spending 30 minutes a week with students, one to one. A commitment of 1 year is considered necessary to develop trust. *Oventes* is the Spanish counterpart. In *Neighbors Involved in Kids' Education (NIKE)*, volunteers provide after-school enrichment in math, science, social studies, communication, physical education, and computers. Projects and activities are designed by the Florida Department of Education. *Safety with Strangers* is a program for children in grades K–5 that uses slides and audio cassettes to teach children how to handle encounters with strangers, to reduce risk of molestation or abduction. In *Superstars,* volunteers work in a program for self-motivated students in grades 1–6 to develop problem-solving skills and creative thinking. *Study Skills Assistants* uses volunteers to train students in study techniques, such as organizing, planning, alphabetizing, and locating information; test taking; and memory devices. Finally, in *Creative Writing,* volunteers work with students on poetry, short stories, and letters, to supplement the creative writing curriculum.

The committee visited four sites in Dade County. At all the sites, committee members were impressed with the warm human involvement of many people in the volunteer programs.

The Southwood Middle School is a school for grades 7–9 in a white upper-middle-class neighborhood that offers instruction in visual arts, photography, literature, and theatre, including dance. The school has many parent support groups that assist in raising money and support for specialty areas and that also help out in class. There is mentoring by senior citizens, and Southwood has several business partners.

Norland Middle School is an arts equivalent of Southwood, in a less affluent neighborhood, which depends primarily on the state department of education program, NIKE. The program uses students from a neighboring high school who work with junior high youngsters in a 2-hour after-school enrichment program in math, science, language arts, computers, and social studies. Sixth graders go to a nearby elementary school to do similar tutoring. The school principal believes Norland's daily attendance rate—the highest in Dade County—is directly due to volunteers' presence and the role modeling of NIKE leaders.

At the Miami Agricultural Center, a retired veterinarian, retired horticulturist, retired carpenters, and retired dog trainer and breeder work with at-risk students to care for and train animals, renovate buildings, and grow plants. The principal of one participating school has done pre- and postprogram research that shows reduced absenteeism and gains in test scores for participating students in comparison with a similar group of students identified as equally at risk but not in the program. All those involved in the program are enthusiastic and convinced that students' emotional and behavior problems have been reduced. "They told me these were pretty tough kids. Around the animals, they turned out to be very enthused and receptive to learning," says a retired veterinarian who spends three afternoons a week "down on the farm."

The Palmetto Elementary School has very high parent and partner participation; the average number of volunteers in the school weekly is 65 to 80, some for all or a major part of the day. It has recouped a declining enrollment through the enthusiastic acceptance of volunteers to work with prekindergarten special education students and emotionally disturbed and nonhandicapped youngsters in grades K–5. The school principal offers strong leadership to the volunteer program; every teacher must have a volunteer. Volunteer programs include a school bank; economics, featuring stocks chosen by students; newspaper writing and editing in cooperation with a local newspaper; library aides; tutors; and a Listeners to Children program for which volunteers are trained by the local mental health association. The principal is fearless in using outside assistance; the school atmosphere is warm and caring.

The committee also met with chairs of the committees and subcommittees of the Miami-Dade advisory committee to the coordinator of community participation, including business representatives, several principals, and a representative of the American Association of Retired Persons. All expressed enthusiastic support for Dade County volunteer activities and were absolutely convinced that their involvement makes an appreciable difference to students and schools.

Existence of an evaluation department in the Dade County public schools has made possible analysis and evaluation of several of the volunteer programs. Probably the best in terms of technical design was the initial

School Volunteer Development Project that ran from 1972 to 1975 with federal funding; a fairly conventional tutoring program that worked with children 1 or more years below grade level in math, reading, or both, it showed relative gains in both math and reading among students.

A second evaluation concerning an adopt-a-grandparent program examined the implementation fidelity of the program and outcomes on both the elderly and children, using a nonequivalent control group design. Positive outcomes were found for attitudes toward the elderly in an at-risk group of children and an increase in self-esteem for at-risk and typical participants in the program. There were no changes for the comparison group of students and no evidence that the program affected the older persons' self-esteem, feelings of depression, or attitudes toward children. There was also an evaluation of the Burger King recognition program, in which students received free food for good attendance and citizenship. It showed strong support in schools and widespread adoption but no evidence that it affected districtwide attendance.

Comet Lab, Adopt-a-Grandparent, and Pet Companion programs were tried simultaneously by a principal on a group of 30 high-risk youths. The evaluation unit conducted a pre- and postprogram analysis, with no comparison group: it showed positive changes in self-concept, self-concept as a learner, and attitudes toward the elderly.

There are two other volunteer-type efforts in Dade County. A program of partnerships between Dade County schools and primarily businesses celebrated its tenth anniversary in 1988. A November 1988 listing showed 183 elementary schools, 48 junior highs, and 41 senior highs and special centers with at least one partner each and some with multiple partners. The total number of partners in Dade County is now reported to be 1,000.

Among the partnership projects is Twiglet Bank, a partnership between First National Bank of South Miami and David Fairchild Elementary School. With the goal of creating an actual bank run by children for children with real money, the First National Bank provided all technical assistance, including training students (a minimum of 2 hours per week per student for 4 months); the cost of renovating a caboose in which the bank is housed; all banking supplies, insurance, security, business cards, and account documentation; and some furniture. The Fairchild School committed to lending whatever school staff support was necessary, in particular by making Twiglet Bank an actual class.

The Bureau of Community Participation also operates a speakers' bureau that invites teachers to request presenters from the community on a wide variety of topics. A catalog provides brief descriptions of the materials that speakers are prepared to present and sets specific procedures, including forms to be used by school staff in requesting and scheduling presentations.

DALLAS, TEXAS

The Dallas Independent School District is the eighth largest in the country, with an enrollment of almost 132,000 students in 181 schools, including 8 magnet high schools and 11 specialized academies or "vanguards" at the elementary and middle school levels. Forty-eight percent of the student population is black, 31 percent Hispanic, 19 percent white, and 2 percent Asian. The school district employs some 10,000 teachers and has an annual budget of $470 million.

In Dallas, parents working through the PTA and other groups were helping in schools even before the district implemented its first official volunteer program in 1969. In that year, the National Council of Jewish Women, followed by Sun Exploration and Production Company and the Junior League of Dallas, began working with the district to provide systematic recruitment, training, and recognition of volunteers. Volunteer participation grew steadily thereafter and increased sharply in 1976 in connection with a desegregation court order. Supporters say the continuing growth of volunteerism is related to local promotion, along with national attention to improving public education.

In 1987–1988, the district reported that 17,325 individual community volunteers worked 411,251 hours; the monetary value of this volunteer service was estimated at $2,878,757. In addition, business volunteers contributed an estimated 35,557 hours, valued at $1,183,090, through adopt-a-school programs and some 2,440 business and school partnerships. All 181 schools have some form of community involvement.

The Dallas school volunteer programs are administered by two paid coordinators who share a position; they are part of the school district's Community Relations Department, which has an annual budget of $5 million. The volunteer office is responsible for training all volunteers who serve in the system, including individuals from the community, parents, and volunteers from adopt-a-school programs and business partnerships. The volunteer office also provides schools with a variety of forms, including a volunteer request form to be completed by teachers, needs assessment forms to be completed by principals to identify specific needs of schools, applications and registration forms to be completed by volunteers, and a volunteer service record for documenting the number of hours contributed by volunteers each month. The office also provides sample letters of appreciation and volunteer appreciation certificates.

At each school in the district, a coordinator, either a member of the staff or a volunteer from the PTA or the community, is responsible for day-to-day volunteer activity, including sign-in of volunteers. The staff volunteer leader or volunteer chairperson at a school is responsible for sending the sign-in sheet to the volunteer office.

The adopt-a-school program is administered separately from the basic volunteer program, though there is considerable cooperation between them. Under the Director of Community Relations and three staff members, the adopt-a-school program is part of an organized effort to supply assistance to individual schools and the district as a whole. Adopters are provided a list of suggested activities, including volunteering and sponsoring special events, and they are urged to select those that match their own capabilities. The adoptions are monitored, and principals are asked at the end of each year to complete an evaluation of the status of the adoption and the degree of involvement by the partners. An effort is made to see that all schools in need receive some form of support.

In counting volunteer service hours from both adopt-a-school and the basic volunteer programs, the Dallas volunteer office takes into account a very long list of activities:

- tutoring;
- a listener program;
- assisting teachers (preparing materials, typing, mimeographing, duplicating, monitoring tests, preparing bulletin boards);
- library work (processing and shelving books, assisting with classes, RIF (Reading Is Fundamental) reading and book distribution, making tape recordings, storytelling, decorating bulletin boards);
- school office assistance (enrollment and pre-enrollment work, answering telephones, attendance monitoring, high school registration, filing, typing, duplicating, clerical assistance);
- classroom enrichment, through SPARK (special programs for enrichment of knowledge, arts and crafts, music, physical education, minicourses);
- lunchroom and playground supervision;
- health room work (18-hour Red Cross training, clinic assistance, special health screening);
- "other school activities" (local school or districtwide volunteer training, sponsoring school club activities, taking pictures of students, assisting assembly programs and classroom parties, interpreting for non-English-speaking parents, orienting new students to school, telephoning parents to check on student attendance, making costumes or scenery, preparing food for student activities or teacher appreciation, helping with senior class activities);
- chaperoning (field trips and local and out-of-town band, orchestra, and choral activities);
- transportation (taking a child other than one's own to a doctor, taking sick children to their homes, driving participants to athletic and other events and contests);

- traffic and bus safety (assisting at safety patrol meetings, monitoring on buses, assisting with loading and unloading buses);
- after-school and summer programs (tutoring hours in summer are counted districtwide unless a particular school is specified);
- volunteer direction (telephoning; attendance at school and volunteer-office-sponsored orientation and training sessions and special workshops; activities related to recruitment, placement, volunteer record-keeping, recognition, etc.);
- workshops (attendance at workshops and training sessions and meetings and individual orientation with teachers and other school personnel);
- community involvement (advisory committee meetings, career counseling, making learning materials at home or school, sponsoring field trips, collecting and disbursing school clothing);
- volunteer executive committee work (assisting volunteer program activities, planning volunteer recognition);
- Dallas City Council of PTA Board of Managers (activities directly affecting students and parents);
- Positive Parents of Dallas (an arm of the PTA that concentrates on providing information to the media); and
- PTA activities, except attendance at board meetings and general meetings.

No fund-raising activities are counted as volunteer hours. In the composite figures for numbers of volunteers, an individual is counted just once, no matter how many incidents of volunteering the individual has been involved in or for how many hours.

In Dallas, committee members visited the Health Special High School for Pregnant Students, where five different sets of volunteers provide a variety of support services to the school and its pregnant students. Volunteers help with intake interviews and clinic and child care services and help the girls resolve problems so they can continue their education after the birth of their babies. Volunteers include seniors from a Catholic high school who tutor; a sorority that provides after-school mentoring; another sorority that operates the Stork's Nest Boutique; the National Council of Jewish Women, which does mentoring and clerical work during school hours; and individuals who tutor students after they return to their home schools. One of the founders of the Dallas school volunteer program 20 years ago is now a regular member of the Pupil Assistance Support Service team at the school.

At a Dallas elementary school, committee members were introduced to "Off Our Rockers" senior citizen volunteers, who tutor 1st graders in reading and help children cut and paste, each with his or her own volunteer. A volunteer from the Dallas Zoo was on hand to give a lecture on snakes, complete with a live example that students could handle. Under an enthusiastic and supportive principal, the elementary school has an adoption with a company, Central and Southwest Services, that "started with dollars and materials and has grown into hands-on people." The company has contributed used computers to the school, and employees instruct youngsters in their use. Also at this school, Highland Park United Methodist Church funds Reading Is Fundamental and supplies volunteers and strong parent support. According to the principal, volunteers "fill the gaps where paid services cannot be supplied." At another elementary school, strong parental support was also evident, in programs run by parents, including an "art cart," music classes, and computer training.

The Junior League of Dallas has developed a special curriculum for non-English-speaking prekindergartners, using props such as groceries on shelves in a simulated store and other commonplace items to engage the youngsters in English-language communication. The "Upwords" program, now in its second year, is expected to ease the transition to regular school for children who do not hear English spoken in their homes. The Dallas Communities in Schools program involves mentors to help motivate students to stay in school and set personal and career goals; and the School Community Guidance Center uses volunteers as resource people for students who need nontraditional settings for education.

Top administrators of the Dallas school system, including a new superintendent who concedes he does not yet have a handle on the multiplicity of volunteer activities going on in his district, are highly supportive of the adopt-a-school and volunteer programs. The district has adopted a policy statement that instructs teachers, principals, and all other staff members to "seek to strengthen and support community groups, cooperating in any way possible to provide assistance, materials, facilities, or other aid to assist them in helping the schools." Each school is to make a systematic effort to identify businesses, industries, other educational institutions, community groups, and organizations that are interested in schools and have resources that would enhance the learning program.

Parents are urged to play a meaningful role in school life, and the district mandates involvement of parents and citizen groups on advisory committees and in other appropriate advisory roles. Principals and teachers are encouraged to be active members of their local Chamber of Commerce and other civic groups that serve the area of the school to which they are assigned.

KINGFIELD, MAINE

Kingfield, Maine, is the headquarters of a rural school district in an isolated area in the western mountains of the state. The district consists of five small towns ranging in size from 550 to just over 1,300 in population, widely scattered over an approximately 400-square-mile area. The population is largely employed in forest products industries and in the recreation business centered on Sugarloaf Mountain. The majority of the parents are high school graduates. However, there are also many professional people in the area and a thriving arts community that organized the Mountain Arts Association that has helped to bring music, painting, performing arts, and dance to the schools. In three-quarters of the families, both parents work.

A little more than 1,000 students are served by four elementary schools and one regional high school. The high school student population was 311 in 1988; the 739 elementary students are roughly divided among four K–8 schools.

The district (Maine School Administrative District No. 58) is governed by a nine-member board of directors and administered by a superintendent. Staffing includes four full-time and one part-time principals and about 66 certified classroom teachers. There are also five special education teachers, two speech therapists, eight Chapter I remedial math and reading teaching assistants, five teacher aides, and one special education teacher's assistant. This small rural district also has a part-time paid volunteer coordinator.

Now more than 10 years old, the district's volunteer program began when a concerned parent saw a need for student enrichment activities and organized volunteer help for the schools with the blessing and support of the school administration. The ski recreation area established on Sugarloaf Mountain Resort had attracted many new families into the area; many of the new residents also saw volunteer work as an avenue for making contacts and establishing friendships in the community, in addition to aiding their children. These parents, as well as longer-time residents, proved willing to contribute time to improve the education of their children.

In December 1979, 89 volunteers were working with the school on a continuing basis in a variety of activities. Parents, grandparents, and some students participated. In time, the volunteer coordinator, originally an unpaid position, became a part-time paid job with support from the school board. Goals for the program were established and became part of a volunteer handbook. In 1983, the state legislature, recognizing the potential contributions of volunteers, passed an act to establish a statewide office of school volunteer programs, and this office now provides support and assistance to volunteer programs throughout the state.

Emphasizing enrichment activities, this rural district has regularly recruited more than 200 people each year, who volunteer about 6,000 hours of time. These numbers probably undercount total volunteers serving the schools: the numbers are derived from sign-up sheets and the hours are those entered in the log each day, but additional services, such as occasional support activities offered by PTA members, are often not recorded and counted.

Parents continued to be the primary source in late 1988, accounting for more than three-fourths of the volunteers. However, services of senior citizens were increasingly tapped, as were young adults (persons with no children in the schools) and students willing to help other students. Some volunteer involvement by local businesses resulted in in-kind contributions: a lumber mill gave drumsticks and furniture; a plant nursery helped kids raise pumpkins; business volunteers put up playgrounds; a paper mill printed note pads with volunteers' names; and one organization set up a portable wildlife exhibit that travels from school to school.

A Junior Great Books program for several levels of elementary students has been operating very successfully since the beginning of the Kingfield volunteer program. This program, requiring the volunteer leaders to be trained by the Great Books Foundation, is a "pull-out" program in which part of an elementary class participates in the enrichment activity, leaving the teacher with a small number of students who can then receive much more individual attention. Other activities in which volunteers play a role include Math Superstars, a math problem-solving activity borrowed, transplanted, and adapted from the Miami Dade County school system; a creative short-story writing activity on the intermediate level; one-on-one tutoring; a gifted and talented program; a German-language program; an art appreciation course; and an active and growing computer activity. Senior volunteers presented a unit on aging and one on World War II. Taking advantage of the fact that the school district is 18 miles from the University of Maine at Farmington, university student volunteers were tapped to help in the School Success Program, which provides support in crafts, recreation, and mentoring for at-risk youngsters. Volunteers also provide clerical and cafeteria support and help in the classroom. The National Dance Institute program brought in by the Mountain Arts Association utilized considerable volunteer help in building scenery, making costumes, and organizing transportation.

PTA activities, including fund raising, are not directly part of the school volunteer program, although there is cooperation and many of the same parents participate in both. During the site visit by the committee (late October 1988), we witnessed a mock election in which students cast ballots for the presidential, state, and local candidates of their choice. This activity, organized by the national PTA, was run by the local PTA and the school volunteer coordinator. Prior to the balloting, students had the opportunity to discuss issues in class and at home with their parents.

Although the volunteer program handbook includes a general statement of goals, specific objectives are program related. For example, the

Junior Great Books program seeks to enhance children's interpretive and communication skills. This program also has its own handbook that spells out teacher, volunteer, and student responsibilities; lays out procedures and materials to be used; and includes an evaluation component by which each group completes an evaluation form at the end of the program.

Needs assessments are conducted informally early in the school year when the volunteer coordinator meets with teachers who request volunteer services, reviews last year's efforts, and discusses volunteer needs for the year ahead. The volunteer coordinator then meets with teachers individually (usually during planning periods) to try and fill specific needs, for example, students who could benefit from one-to-one tutoring in reading and math. Because the district is small, the volunteer coordinator personally knows all of the teachers and the volunteers.

Recruitment of volunteers is one of the duties of the volunteer coordinator. A form is taken home by each child at the beginning of the school year asking if parents want to volunteer. Lists of possible tasks accompany the form, which gives the parent an idea of what help is needed. Inasmuch as the program is now more than 10 years old, there is a core of persons who volunteer each year, so the recruitment effort is to replace those whose children have left school or who go to work or stop for some other reason. In addition, the coordinator frequently calls persons who are on the substitute teacher list, who will often volunteer if no work is available. A newsletter describing what is going on and requesting help needed also serves as a recruitment vehicle. Again, because each town is small, specific needs can often be met by word-of-mouth recruitment. Someone usually knows someone who can handle a particular task. Future plans call for attempting to get greater involvement from fathers and from local businesses.

Although the program is run informally, there are administrative procedures that govern operation of the program. Volunteers are required to sign in and out in a log book when they work at each of the schools. Procedures are explained during orientation sessions set up if there are many new volunteers or done individually, often together with the teacher the volunteer will be helping, if turnover is small and few new recruits come into the program. Screening of new volunteers is done, but subtly so as not to offend anyone. Tuberculin tests are required every 2 years. If a prospective volunteer is not suited to work with students or does not want to do so, the volunteer coordinator usually tries to find work that he or she can do at home. Again, because the community is small, most people know each other and it is seldom that a complete stranger is screened. Assignments are made on the basis of the volunteers' interests and skills, beginning with what they noted on the sign-up sheets. Job or task descriptions are usually informal and set forth by the teacher and volunteer coordinator, particularly if the volunteer effort is to be more than short term.

Formal training is offered only when a particular program requires it. The Junior Great Books program does have specific training requirements for volunteers who participate in the program, and the school district pays for people to participate in the training conducted by the Great Books Foundation. Teachers also receive formal training when needed, but usually are informally instructed by the volunteer coordinator as to their responsibilities with respect to the volunteers who help them.

Because of the nature of the area, volunteers usually stay for several years, particularly while they have children in elementary and intermediate grades. Recognition for volunteer efforts takes many forms. Name recognition is possible through the volunteer program newsletter; social events (e.g., breakfasts, ice cream socials) are also used to acknowledge the contribution of volunteers.

Much of the assessment of volunteer programs is conducted on an informal basis. The coordinator is in frequent touch with teachers in each school, and they discuss how the programs are going and any problems that need resolution or improvement. There is also an annual evaluation form completed by all teachers who use volunteers. This form uses a 4-point rating scale to rate service performed, and it includes some 21 questions aimed at getting teacher's perceptions as to accomplishments of the program, as well as suggestions for improvement. A similar form is completed by each volunteer. The coordinator reviews all forms as an additional aid to determining what works best and what improvements are needed. A separate evaluation is made for the Junior Great Books program, and students also complete an evaluation form for this program.

Perceptions as to what could be done to improve the program include greater community involvement, particularly by fathers and businesses in the area. More and better training for volunteers and the teachers who use them could result in even better programs. Those few instances in which the use of volunteers did not work out well were almost always due to insufficient knowledge of what was expected or to insufficient training. Impediments to carrying out successful programs are chiefly insufficient funds for training and for materials and transportation.

MONTGOMERY COUNTY, MARYLAND

The Montgomery County School Volunteer Program has been in operation since August 1978. The program serves a large, diverse county with a population of 650,000, bordering on Washington, D.C. The county has been described as a relatively well-to-do suburban community, a bedroom community for the nation's capital. Actually, the county includes

considerable light industry—research and other white-collar services—
and it includes urban and rural as well as suburban areas. In 1987–1988,
there were 161 public schools administered as one district by a superintendent under an elected school board. There were close to 100,000 public
school students and 6,833 teachers. Approximately 67 percent of the students were white and 33 percent minority (15.6 percent black, 10.6 percent
Asian, 6.6 percent Hispanic, and 0.2 percent Native American).

The county school volunteer program was organized as a result of a
relatively low-key state initiative beginning in the middle 1970s. During
that period the state superintendent had applied for and received a federal grant under the Education Professions Development Act to fund a
staff specialist in volunteer program development. That specialist invited
school superintendents from all over the state to send representatives to a
round-table meeting on developing volunteer programs. After this initial
meeting, the representative from Montgomery County was particularly
interested in reading improvement programs that were organized by volunteers with help from a number of PTAs. These efforts proved successful enough that the Board of Education allocated one half-time position in
each of the county's six areas to bolster reading and to organize volunteers to help. The tight money situation in 1975–1976 resulted in cutbacks
on these positions, and the volunteer program, with no one to continue to
organize and keep it going, began to fade.

Recognizing the contributions possible from volunteer help, one county
school board member pushed for and succeeded in establishing a full-
time position in 1978 for a coordinator of volunteer services to serve the
county. With someone in charge and responsible, this program grew rapidly over the next 10 years. By 1988 the volunteer services staff of two
professionals and a part-time secretary (a budget under $100,000) had
recruited and placed 29,187 volunteers who provided 1,691,049 hours of
services to students and teachers in grades K–12, Head Start, and adult
education. About 7,000 of these volunteers worked in instructional programs; more than 12,000 served school support needs; and another 10,000
provided occasional services as speakers, contest judges, and so on.

Volunteers helping with instruction served an average of 3 hours per
week as classroom aides, tutors, mentors, tutors in English for speakers of
other languages, computer assistants, media center aides, and career education assistants. In support services, volunteers averaged 2.5 hours per
week working as chaperons and room parents, boosters, advisory committee members, newsletter editors, clerical and attendance aides, and
health room and cafeteria aides.

To manage this program, the volunteer services coordinator works
closely with each school participating in the volunteer program. Volunteer program coordination at the school building level is provided by

volunteers recruited by the PTA and appointed by the principal. These coordinators team up with paid staff at the school to provide administrative management of the program; they recruit, orient, screen, place, and provide recognition for volunteers, while the paid staff coordinator (usually a part-time teacher or administrator) provides faculty orientation, conducts a staff needs assessment, and coordinates the training and supervision of volunteers. The training given volunteers averages only 3.8 hours per year but is considered essential to their effective utilization. Both paid and volunteer program coordinators, and the volunteers themselves, participate in the evaluation of the program.

The central office coordinator of volunteer services conducts twice-yearly volunteer program management training for both paid and volunteer staff. A course for teachers is also offered—"The Effective Use of Volunteer Services in the Classroom." The course is approved by the Maryland State Department of Education for 1 hour of credit for recertification. In addition, the central office of volunteer services provides handbooks, forms, certificates, and other program materials to schools.

The volunteer services coordinator also is on call to provide consultant services in program development to principals and PTA representatives. In addition to school recognition activities, the Board of Education holds a yearly reception to honor the principals, volunteer coordinators, and volunteers of programs that meet the State Department of Education criteria for an outstanding program. These criteria specify a staff orientation program in which a minimum of 80 percent of the staff has participated; an individual (either staff or volunteer) designated to provide training, leadership, and coordination to the school volunteer program; and a corps of volunteers who provide an average of not less than 100 hours per year of volunteer services in the school instructional program per each 50 students in the school. To encourage high schools and other schools that are just beginning their volunteer programs, a showing of 50 percent more volunteer hours than the previous year can be substituted for this last requirement. In 1988, 71 schools were honored.

In addition to the school-organized volunteer programs, the Office of Volunteer Services offers teachers the Connection Resource Bank (CRB), a computerized data base of volunteered resources to support the mathematics and science curriculum in grades K–12. The CRB is a project of the Montgomery Education Connection, a nonprofit foundation of local businesses whose mission is to support public education in Montgomery County. Teachers can obtain information about personnel, site resources, materials, and educational opportunities for themselves through a phone call to the CRB. In three years of operation, the CRB filled 1,158 teacher requests and served 31,391 students.

Volunteers are recruited from various groups in the community, but the preponderance, 82 percent, are parents. Given the small central office staff and the school-based volunteer organization, this emphasis could be predicted. Business volunteers account for 8 percent, community organizations about 6 percent, senior citizens 3 percent, and college and university students only about 1 percent of volunteers. The dollar value of the hours provided by volunteers, if estimated using the low hourly wage of school aides, would still be in excess of $11 million according to the volunteer services coordinator. This figure represents an increase of 2 percent in the school budget, or the equivalent of 813 full-time, 12-month staff people.

Support for the volunteer program from the superintendent and the school board is solid. Involvement of the community is considered essential for a good school program, and extensive use of volunteers who have first-hand knowledge of their school is a major factor in organizing this community support. Principals are encouraged to organize volunteer programs in their schools.

To aid in monitoring the volunteer programs, a survey of volunteer services is conducted each year. The survey forms are completed at each school (using volunteer services), based on compilations from sign-in sheets that volunteers fill in each time they work. The detail compiled provides a comprehensive picture of numbers of volunteers, hours worked, type of activity, school level, and training conducted, as well as respondents' comments on major strengths of the program, major needs, and services they would like the central office to provide. Individual reports are used to review what is happening at each school; the data are also compiled for the entire district and used to monitor progress. A summary report is sent to the state office.

Because of the small staff, little effort is spent on determining the accuracy of each school's report. Qualifying for the state honors, for example, is an inducement to record-keeping, which could also lead to overstating numbers, but volunteers who occasionally drop in to a school for a few hours may not sign in and are frequently not included in the volunteer count.

Evaluation forms are aimed at obtaining individual teacher and volunteer perceptions of the program's effectiveness. They are used chiefly in monitoring the process and to pinpoint problems that need attention. Growth of the volunteer program and greater willingness of teachers and administrators to participate are pointed to as indications of program success. Formal evaluations on outcomes have not been attempted.

SAN FERNANDO VALLEY, CALIFORNIA

The volunteer program visited by the committee in the San Fernando Valley area of Los Angeles County is different than those we visited in other cities. Known as the 31st District Parent-Teacher-Student Association (PTSA), the volunteer organization is a nonprofit group that operates independently of the Los Angeles Unified School District. It is administered by a 16-member volunteer corporate board of directors elected by delegates from its membership of 76,000. Its mission is to benefit all children; its focus is on the students attending the Los Angeles public schools in its area; and it is recognized under board rules of the Los Angeles Unified School District.

The San Fernando Valley area of Los Angeles (the 31st District) includes 171 schools and 168,000 students. The volunteer organization has two distinctive functions. As an entity established in 1953 by the California State PTA, it is authorized to carry out its programs and facilitate the administration of 152 units and membership within seven PTA councils in the San Fernando Valley, County of Los Angeles. The objectives of the PTA are promoted through educational endeavors directed toward parents, teachers, and the general public, and they are developed through conferences, committees, projects, and programs. Under its Articles of Incorporation in the State of California, its primary purposes include carrying on philanthropic and educational work and promoting the welfare of children and youth in the home, school, community, and place of worship. This was the impetus to create and administer programs cooperatively designed to meet the needs of the students of the Los Angeles Unified School District.

The concept of volunteerism within the 31st District PTSA is unique in that volunteer professionals design and administer programs or projects for which staff may be employed to implement. No member of the PTSA board may be employed by the PTSA. Dedicated volunteers contributed nearly 20,000 hours to PTSA projects in 1987–1988.

The 31st District PTSA volunteers develop policies and procedures to ensure compliance with all applicable federal, state, and local regulations as to legal and financial accountability for staffing, certification, insurance, leasing, and licensing. Each project or program is evaluated individually on an annual basis and should be self-sustaining. Grants to maintain financial viability may be considered.

The socioeconomic composition of the population of the area served by the PTSA programs and projects ranges from poverty level to upper middle class. According to the Los Angeles Unified School District, the schools in the area include those that are overcrowded and operate year round in addition to those with a traditional calendar; the students are about 15 percent white, 63 percent Hispanic, and the rest other minority. The population served by the PTSA projects that the committee visited are primarily minority children from single-parent families or families where both parents are employed and unable to afford private care.

Many programs and projects are administered by the 31st District PTSA.

Three were reviewed by the committee: PTA Latchkey Project, PTA dental clinics, and PTA health clinics. In the PTA Latchkey Project, nearly 90 employees provide affordable, quality care at 17 school sites, before and after school, for approximately 800 elementary students, of whom 25 percent are subsidized (partly by a United Way allocation). The PTA dental clinics program employs a dentist to operate three clinics year round and several dentists and dental technicians to serve students otherwise unable to afford dental care (subsidized in part by United Way); there were more than 5,000 visits for dental care in 1988–1989. Of the PTA health clinics, two are operated in conjunction with the Los Angeles Unified School District, for which the 31st District PTSA employs optometrists and ophthalmologists, who dispensed over 1,000 new glasses to students in 1988–1989.

The PTA Latchkey Project began as a pilot project in 1982 in response to a needs survey conducted by the 31st District PTSA in the communities that it serves. A lack of affordable, supervised activities for elementary school students before and after school was identified. Concerns were expressed about gangs, drugs, and poverty and the need for this service in a secure environment.

Using a combination of persistence, acquired expertise, and volunteer efforts, leases were obtained for space in school buildings from the school district and licenses were obtained from the Department of Social Services for three sites. Having pioneered this venture successfully, the PTA worked for the passage of child care legislation. In 1985, California enacted legislation, SB 303, that made state funds available to public and private agencies to operate latchkey centers in schools. The Los Angeles Unified School District (LAUSD) applied for and received funds to establish other sites. Subsequently, the mayor of Los Angeles, the City Council, and businesses have supplemented funding for additional programs in the district.

Parents or guardians may enroll children who are students at the school at which the PTA Latchkey Program is offered for a fee; 25 percent are subsidized. Each site has a director who must have a minimum of 12 college units in child development, a counselor with a minimum of 6 units, and an aide. An adult/child ratio of at least 1:12 is maintained. Each program in the project must provide time for homework, with tutoring if necessary; some physical activity; some opportunity for quiet play; and nutritious refreshments. Each program may offer enrichment activities requested by parents. Each center has facilities for children who are ill.

Each year the PTA Latchkey Project conducts a survey of parents and summarizes the responses. In June 1988, the project reported five positive responses for every concern or suggestion. Among the criticisms, parents wanted either more or less structure, longer program hours, chocolate milk or no chocolate milk, more adults per student, more supervision but not a "prison," more or less organized play, more artwork, more exercise or dance, quiet time instead of naps, more parent involvement, more security, and isolation for children with colds. At every site, parents asked for more help with homework. Concerns and suggestions have prompted program refinement.

Overall, the income of the project currently exceeds expenses. Salaries and benefits have been increased for site employees; an increase in subsidized fees will be explored; and an executive administrator may be employed due to project expansion and to relieve routine project administrative responsibilities of the Board of Directors.

At the PTA health centers, in addition to the optometric services and eyeglasses provided by PTAs and PTSAs, diagnostic services including cardiology, otology, neurology, audiometry, orthopedics, weight control, pediatrics, and general medicine are mostly provided by the staff of the Los Angeles Unified School District.

Students must be referred to the PTA health centers by a school nurse, doctor, or administrator; parents or guardians may make appointments at the PTA dental clinics for any student in the Los Angeles schools. Forty percent of the cost of the dental services rendered is underwritten by contributions from PTA or PTSA units within the 31st District and by a grant from United Way. Fees are calculated on the balance, and charges are also subject to a social services scale based on the family's size and income. Any remaining portion that the family is unable to pay is either paid by the school's PTA or PTSA unit or with funds from a PTSA reserve account.

Los Angeles Unified School District personnel, from the area superintendent to the president of the Board of Education to the site principals, consider the PTA Latchkey Project and PTA dental and health clinics a critical support system for educators and suggest that it may be necessary to redefine the role of schools in urban areas to include such services.

Despite the complexities of operating what is in effect a social service agency, the PTSA is expanding its services. Three of the original founding members of the PTA Latchkey Project who met with the committee said they view the PTSA's involvement in out-of-school supplemental activities as being within the purview of PTA's mission.

SAN FRANCISCO, CALIFORNIA

The San Francisco Unified School District (SFUSD) represents a compact urban area of about 700,000 people, where living and especially housing costs are among the highest in the country. In 1988, there were 114 public schools serving approximately 65,000 students, including 14 ethnic groups with 27 different languages. More than one-half of San Francisco's school children come from homes in which English is not the primary language. Eighty percent of the school students are defined as having special needs; almost 35 percent are limited in English proficiency; about 15 percent come from homes receiving welfare; and 85 percent are minorities.

With tight budgets characteristic of most of the nation's large cities, San Francisco's teacher/student ratio is 1:32 for the K–12 grades and it is one of the highest in the country. Nevertheless, according to the superintendent, emphasis is on individualized instruction for each student, placing heavy demands on classroom teachers. The committee was told that teachers are increasingly reaching out to the volunteer community for help not only in broadening and enriching their students' education but also to ensure that each student can adequately read, write, and compute.

The task of recruiting, screening, training, and placing these volunteers is the responsibility of the San Francisco School Volunteers, an independent nonprofit agency. Begun in 1962 by two volunteers who assisted with reading and story telling in two schools, the agency (then known as the San Francisco Education Auxiliary) boosted its number of volunteers to 30 in 1963 and received some initial support from the school district. By 1966 the organization had expanded to 200 volunteers working in 16 schools; and by 1970 the number had tripled to 620 volunteers working in elementary, junior high, and high schools. By the mid- and late 1970s, this organization, maintaining its organizational structure as a nonprofit independent group working closely with the school district and with continued but modest support, had expanded to four citywide projects, including a cross-age tutoring program and a speakers' bureau, and had placed about 2,000 volunteers working in schools. In this period the first business involvement program was established, a program that has continued to the present. In the late 1970s, special projects were initiated to provide English tutoring help for immigrant children, to involve senior citizens, and to assist handicapped and disabled children. During this period the agency also began to build teacher training into the program. The independent organization changed its name to the San Francisco School Volunteers in the early 1980s.

New programs continued to be added, including a foreign-language enrichment program and a math program designed to improve students' problem-solving abilities. By the middle and late 1980s, the agency had extended its involvement in literacy issues and had launched, with the support of the superintendent, an adopt-a-school business program matching individual businesses with schools in a partnership relationship. As of 1988, the agency's annual report showed operation of 11 programs in the city, serving some 33,000 students and 2,100 teachers, with more than 2,200 volunteers in all 114 of the city's schools.

To provide these services, the San Francisco School Volunteers has a paid staff of 17 professional and clerical employees. It is managed by a director, is governed by a board of directors, and has an active advisory committee that provides direction to the board with more than 60 members serving on project committees. The annual budget is close to $500,000, with funding provided through grants from a number of foundations, donations from corporations, and special fund-raising events, as well as the contribution of the school district. In addition to managing the program, the director must be active in fund raising from corporations and must develop proposals for funds from foundations and from federal, state, and local government agencies.

The independent organization of the San Francisco School Volunteers allows for considerable creativity in designing projects and raising funds to implement them. However, such funding is usually short term, requiring continuous fund-raising activity and a constant effort to persuade a tight-budgeted school system to take over funding so that successful projects can continue and be expanded to all schools in the system.

Working relationships with the school district are described as very close, with the volunteer organization helping the schools to determine their needs and then attempting to recruit volunteers to fill them. Support from the superintendent is enthusiastic, there is written policy support for volunteer activities, and part of the evaluation of school principals depends on how well they have used volunteers. The superintendent, expressing his own views, said that major changes in the U.S. education systems must include the involvement of the community in a structured, organized way to supplement organized teaching. Economics, for example, should be taught not only by a teacher but with help from volunteers from the banking community or other experts.

Projects developed by the agency are consistent with goals set by the school district and in support of needs determined by individual schools. The central, and by far the largest, activity of the volunteer organization is the recruitment and training of volunteers to meet the needs of each school. These needs range from tutorial help for reading and math, to help for learning disabled students, to music and art enrichment activities. Volunteers are recruited from school parents, the community, and citywide. Parents constitute the largest source, but senior citizens, university students, and business people also provide volunteer services. The volunteer organization does the recruiting, interviewing, and placing of volunteers. It not only helps each school in encouraging parents and others in the community to become involved, but also recruits directly through extensive media outreach to local newspapers, radio, and television stations; close working relationships with local and out-of-state university programs; contacts with area community, ethnic, professional, and educational organizations; and through use of the organization's advisory committee. The agency also offers training both in one-on-one tutoring and in understanding and working with students from diverse cultures and provides consultant services, including training and helping school volunteer coordinators in developing strategies for involving parents and other community volunteers in school programs and activities.

Special programs designed with the aid of educational experts and usually funded by foundations or corporations are also in operation to help implement school district goals. These include experimental programs in math, reading and language arts, special education, and critical thinking and writing. All of these programs have stated goals and objectives and provide for a strong evaluation component measuring student achievement, self-esteem, and other outcomes, as well as assessing the effectiveness of the process by which the achievements were accomplished.

Several programs are specifically aimed at involving the business community as well as parents. For example, the Think/Write Program, teams professional writers from major San Francisco area corporations with teachers in middle and high school classrooms. The objective is to give students a realistic view of the importance of critical thinking and to develop practical and creative writing skills ranging from letters, memos, press releases, and job applications to short stories and movie reviews. The activity is highly organized, with both teachers and volunteers participating in considerable training. The teams usually do the writing assignments themselves before they are presented in class, and they use such techniques as brainstorming, mind-mapping, revising, editing, and group criticism to expose students to the importance of critical thinking as well as creativity. Viewed skeptically at first by teachers, the program, now in its third year, has more applicants than can be accommodated.

Other programs include creative ways of enriching the language arts curriculum with quality literature, training senior citizen volunteers in teaching English as a second language so that they can tutor the large number of immigrant students, and helping elementary school children understand and accept children with disabilities. Business partnerships, including the Adopt-A-School program, not only bring volunteers to the schools but provide resources such as management workshops for school administrators, scholarships, summer job opportunities, and other support for students, teachers, and schools.

Making it possible for experimental programs that have been proven successful to be introduced in schools that have not been part of the experiment is a major challenge for the school district. Some of these projects, such as the Think/Write Program, are literally changing the way critical thinking and writing are taught in the participating schools. Finding ways after foundation funding runs out to continue this creative collaboration of teachers and business volunteers and to provide the training required to assure the success of this type of program adds to the school district's challenge.

Evaluation of virtually all aspects of volunteer activity is carried out or supported by the San Francisco School Volunteers. For example, each school year separate evaluation forms are completed by volunteer coordinators in each school and by the volunteers. The questions cover perceptions of usefulness of volunteers and allow for comments on the role of the volunteer organization in recruiting, placing, training, and monitoring. Summary data show a generally high level of satisfaction. Individual comments, however, have indicated trouble spots in communication, training, and inadequate orientation at the school or lack of understanding on the part of the teacher as to how to use a volunteer's time effectively, and they have been used to remedy problems. Overall, forms returned by the volunteers also indicate a high level of satisfaction.

In addition to the evaluation forms from volunteer coordinators and volunteers, each project funded by foundation or corporate sources has stated goals and objectives and a built-in evaluation aspect. These evaluations, usually conducted by outside experts, include, as appropriate, assessment of academic achievement as well as indications of self-esteem, reduction of absenteeism, and attitude changes of students and teachers. Evaluation results show substantial improvements in elementary reading scores, high school foreign-language scores, and noticeable gains in student problem-solving ability in mathematics, writing, and English. Contributions of volunteers toward reading improvement score measurements made before and after volunteer programs are implied. The extent to which improvements are due to better teaching or to help from the volunteers could not be measured, but the improvements were clearly there, and teachers attested to the contributions of the volunteers.

TULSA, OKLAHOMA

The Tulsa, Oklahoma, school system has lost more than one-half of its students in the past decade, as a result of sharp declines in the oil economy. Currently, 41,000 students attend the district's 78 elementary, middle, and high schools. More than two-thirds of the students are white, one-third are black, and a number are Native American. In Tulsa, most black families live in one part of the city, whites in another.

The Tulsa community is traditionally conservative, with an orientation to solving its own problems. While the city has pockets of poverty, disadvantage looks different in Tulsa than it does in densely populated cities such as Chicago and Los Angeles. Neighborhoods described as among the poorest were generally made up of single-family homes with lawns, orderly and well maintained.

An extremely strong and comprehensive school volunteer program in Tulsa had its roots in a 1970s school desegregation effort, when Tulsa, determined to avoid court-ordered desegregation, created a voluntary system of magnet schools with heavy parent involvement. In addition, under its current superintendent, the school system is committed to "effective schools" principles, including community involvement. In the 1987–1988 school year, between 3,900 and 4,000 volunteers worked in Tulsa schools, contributing approximately 169,000 hours of service in a variety of capacities ranging from direct involvement in the instructional process to clerical support for teachers and administrative staff.

The climate appears to favor school volunteerism and community involvement in Tulsa, but without exception the school officials we met during a 2-day visit to Tulsa credited an individual, the director of business/community resources, with the effectiveness of the district's volunteer and partnership programs. The director was active as a parent in the magnet school desegregation plan, became the first director of school volunteers in Tulsa in the early 1970s, and now administers an Adopt-a-School business partnership program, as well as an array of specialized volunteer programs developed to meet specific needs of the schools and students.

During the committee's Tulsa visit, we met with the superintendent and with the associate superintendent for instruction. Both expressed unequivocal support for the Business/Community Resources program. Two teacher union representatives with whom we met were equally supportive. The president and vice-president of the Tulsa Classroom Teachers Association said teachers in Tulsa are enthusiastic about having volunteer assistance. Asked if volunteers are seen as performing jobs that might otherwise go to paid aides, one said: "As I see it, volunteers are doing things that would not be done at all if they were not in the schools." The teacher representatives indicated some preference for corporate volunteers, saying they tend to be less intrusive and less emotional about school operations than parent volunteers.

On a schedule that began at 8 a.m. each day, we visited six schools, each with a volunteer program that represents one approach to community involvement. In each school, volunteer activities were organized and structured and addressed specific instructional objectives.

McLain High School is in a predominantly black neighborhood in one of the city's lowest-income areas. The school is bright, clean, and orderly, and the students are well dressed and personable. The principal is using many techniques to persuade neighborhood children to remain at McLain and not transfer to one of the city's magnet high schools. Recently, he and the district coordinator developed an Adopt-a-Class project in which professionals, most of them black, come into classes on a regular basis to talk about student problems or about their own careers and educational experiences. On the day of our visit, a college admissions officer was discussing student aid with a class of seniors; a husband-and-wife team was leading a discussion of drug abuse and suicide; and a dentist was describing tooth structure. Many of the volunteers were on released time from area businesses and corporations. The volunteers meet once a month to exchange information and make plans; according to the principal, they provide invaluable role models for his students.

At Houston Elementary School, there is an active Take Reading to Heart program in which community volunteers (at Houston the volunteers were Junior Leaguers) work one on one with kindergarteners and 1st graders who are having reading difficulties. The volunteers use a variety of objects, including letter shapes and picture cards, to determine if the children have necessary reading readiness skills and to remedy deficiencies. At some point in the session, each child gets to snuggle into a cushioned area to read a book with a tutor. According to the school principal, the program has significantly reduced the number of children who must spend a developmental year between kindergarten and 1st grade.

At Sequoyah Elementary School we talked with a counselor who approached the district coordinator with a request for adult friends for the increasing number of students in Sequoyah's middle-class community whose parents work or are otherwise unable to give their children time and companionship. In this program, students from a nearby college walk to the elementary school, and a partnership has been developed in which the college students come to school regularly to talk with their young friends, walk with them on the school grounds, or help with a school project. We were presented with letters written for us by some of the students about "the best, best friend I ever had." Students are suggested for the program by their teachers and must have parental permission to participate.

Cleveland Middle School, which enrolls students from a middle-class working community and has a large number of Native American students, has been adopted by Warren Petroleum Company. Evidence of the partnership includes computers in the media center, volunteers from the company who teach computer use, and the library's recently computerized records, which were accomplished with volunteer help. The adoption is clearly mutual: the assistant principal pointed to a trophy case of students' artwork saluting their business partner.

At Lindbergh Elementary School, volunteers are an integral part of kindergarten every day. The committee found it hard to tell which of the adults in the three kindergarten sections were staff and which were volunteers. The volunteers are essential to the teacher's program, in which children are busy with many different activities at the same time. Volunteers were clearly comfortable with their roles, helping with paints, pinning up artwork, smiling with approval, or clearing up spills. As in the other Tulsa schools visited, the volunteers appeared to be well oriented and trained and went about their activities with confidence.

The Disney Elementary School uses volunteers in a science enrichment program developed for the Tulsa schools by scientists at Amoco research headquarters in Tulsa. The scientists developed a hands-on curriculum in which students work in small groups to perform experiments and solve problems. The curriculum, now distributed nationally, relies explicitly on volunteers to work with the students. According to the science teacher, the volunteers often contribute creative ideas of their own to enhance the program. At the time of the committee's visit, students were clearly absorbed and engaged in learning under competent volunteer supervision. Disney Elementary School also has other volunteer programs, including a volunteer workroom, where teachers can leave requests for copying, laminating, or other small services; volunteers pick up the requests when they arrive at school and fill them. As at the other Tulsa schools, the volunteers seemed exceptionally well organized and self-starting.

Tulsa's Adopt-a-School program, begun 5 years ago, is a joint effort between the Tulsa Board of Education and the Metropolitan Tulsa Chamber of Commerce. Companies and organizations are asked to be committed for a full year and to release their employees in teams for up to 3 hours a week. Principals and teachers are expected to design programs linking students with volunteers, and the district school volunteer coordinator keeps communication open among the participants and assures that the objectives of each are being met. Schools are encouraged to assess their needs and request adoption on the basis of those needs. After adoption, the Business/Community Resource program staff conducts an orientation for school personnel and the adopting partner. Once the program is in place, a written evaluation is completed by participants at the end of each year.

One staff member in the four-person Business/Community Resource Office spends full time managing a Volunteer Speakers Bureau. A list of speaker topics starts with "Acting," "Accounting," "Adoption," "Aerospace," and "Agriculture" and ends with "Welding," "Wildlife," "Wills and Trusts," "Word Processing," "Writers," and "Zoo." Teachers may request the services of a speaker by mailing a speaker request form to the office, detailing such items as the purpose of the presentation, the instructional unit or activity to which it relates, the grade level, and the number of students. The speaker is identified and confirmed to the teacher and principal. Both the teacher and the speaker receive guidelines for presentations, and the speaker receives an introduction card and name tag. Teachers are asked to complete an evaluation form after the event, and speakers are officially thanked by the Business/Community Resource Office.

WASHINGTON, D.C.

Washington, D.C., is the 15th largest city in the nation. The estimated population in 1988 was 621,658. According to a survey conducted by the Greater Washington Research Center in 1986, the population was 67 percent black, 28 percent white, and 5 percent "other races." Washington is also one of the most culturally and linguistically diverse cities in the United States. It is also a city of extreme contrasts. According to the 1980 census, more than 28 percent of the residents above 25 had attended 4 or more years of college, yet almost 16 percent had not completed elementary school. More than 14 percent of the households lived in poverty, yet the District had the second highest per capita income in the nation.

The 1988 student enrollment stands at 87,700, including 51,174 elementary students (prekindergarten through grade 6); 17,196 junior high students (grades 7–9); 17,396 senior high students (grades 10–12); and 1,080 students in special education. The school system also serves approximately 18,000 residents citywide with adult education services. Of the 1988 prekindergarten through 12th grade enrollment, 96 percent of the students are minorities, of which 91.7 percent are black. In 1989–1990, the public school enrollment is expected to be 90,200. For the school year 1988–1989, there were 19,805 D.C. resident students attending private schools, about the same number as in 1987.

According to the Division of Bilingual Education Fact Sheet dated November 30, 1988, the language minority student enrollment in the school system is 8,991, a growth of 6,500 students from the 1980 level of 2,400. Recently, a substantial number of students from Central and South America, Asia, North Africa, and the Caribbean islands moved to Washington. Such a diverse student population has complex cultural, linguistic, and educational needs. The largest concentration, Hispanic, represents every Spanish-speaking country in the world, with a great number of students from El Salvador, Guatemala, Nicaragua, the Dominican Republic, and Mexico.

The school administrative structure is unique, as might be expected for the city. One superintendent and one Board of Education execute what are, elsewhere, both state and local district functions. The first elected school board was established in 1968; the first nonvoting student member of the board was elected in 1982.

Washington was one of the cities that received seed money from the National School Volunteer Program of the Public Education Association of New York City in the mid-1970s to establish a school volunteer program. Under an energetic superintendent, the city continued to expand its community involvement and now operates comprehensive school volunteer, Adopt-a-School, and partnership programs, all administered by a

Volunteer Services and Training Branch established in 1977. In the 1987–1988 school year, the school system reported that 23,007 volunteers gave 5 million hours of time, worth $25 million; and every one of the city's 200 schools and programs received some kind of volunteer service. Fifty-one percent of volunteers serve in elementary schools, 20 percent in middle and junior high schools, 10 percent in high schools, 13 percent in adult education, 12 percent in special education, and 4 percent in community schools.

Volunteer efforts fall into four major categories: support to instruction, which includes tutoring and classroom assistance (53 percent); extension services, defined as additions to counseling or administrative functions (17 percent); enrichment activities in the form of extracurricular learning experiences (21 percent); and advisory and advocacy activities (9 percent).

The school board has established detailed regulations for the utilization of volunteer services. The superintendent and staff are specifically authorized to accept such services provided that no volunteer performs "any function or service that is currently being performed by an employee" and voluntary services or their availability are not used as a basis for "reduction in force" of school personnel. Volunteers are required to sign a statement acknowledging that they have been informed of the nature and scope of the voluntary services to be performed and of the board's regulations, especially those concerning confidentiality, conflict of interest, liability protection, and political activity.

The Volunteer Services and Training Branch conducts districtwide recruiting and volunteer recognition and is available to schools for technical assistance in program development, volunteer training, and staff development. The branch also provides guest speakers for schools or community groups and materials to support tutorial instruction and related efforts. Schools are also encouraged to recruit their own volunteers. A coordinator is appointed for each building by the principal; this is usually a resource teacher or assistant principal. The coordinator collects and reports volunteer names and hours and serves as liaison with the branch for training and other assistance.

The Volunteer Services and Training Branch also administers a number of districtwide programs that provide volunteers to schools. They include Operation Rescue, an elementary tutorial program cosponsored by the Washington Urban League; Project Mentor, a secondary mentoring program using volunteer professionals to supplement counseling services; Operation Outreach, an after-school tutorial program for secondary students; and Project Access, a pre-employment training program for high school seniors. The branch also assists schools to set up partnerships with businesses, community organizations, or government agencies.

The committee's visit included a half-day briefing at the offices of the

Volunteer Services and Training Branch by the director. Meetings were also held with the executive assistant to the superintendent for corporate liaison and with a member of the Board of Education, both of whom were highly supportive of the volunteer and partnership programs. The assistant to the superintendent said that schools are looking to the community for technical support, since even highly trained teachers have limited competence in areas out of their discipline. He noted that the district is asking businesses, "How is it you instruct your employees, and is it applicable to schools?" The board member stressed the importance of parent and community involvement in schools in her ward.

We visited three schools, one elementary, one junior high, and one senior high, all with active volunteer programs. Stevens Elementary School was built in 1868 as one of the first school for blacks in the District of Columbia and was named for Pennsylvania Congressman Thadeus Stevens. It is located in the heart of D.C.'s high-rise financial district. The school's attendance area includes the White House, but children attend from all over Washington in part because of an extended-day program that enables parents who work to pick their children up as late as 6 p.m. The principal has turned the school's midtown location to advantage: "I walk into the offices and say, 'We need help'," she said.

On the day of our visit, a federal judge was challenging teams of 5th graders to compete in answering general-knowledge questions; he comes to the school weekly. A brokerage firm has developed a stock market program using math and reading skills; children follow the progress of stocks in daily newspapers, plan investment strategies, and make or lose "money." At the end of the year, the firm provides each child one share of stock. Teachers spoke with enthusiasm about volunteers in their building and noted that many children develop close friendships with volunteer mentors and tutors. The children at Stevens seemed completely at ease with visitors; they were friendly and self-confident, as were the faculty.

Our visit to Shaw Junior High was in the afternoon after classes had ended; we therefore saw no students or volunteers, but the coordinators of the school's volunteer program and a community education program that uses volunteers gave us a comprehensive briefing. Shaw, once notorious for violence and disorder, is a tightly controlled campus; students are not allowed to leave school during the day, and cleanliness and order are rigorously maintained. Parents are required to come to the school when students have problems and to take responsibility for their children's behavior and achievement.

Shaw has numerous adopters, including a major chain of food markets, and is partnered with McDonalds, J.W. Marriott, and IBM. In 1987 the school celebrated "A Decade of Volunteer Service in an Inner-City School," including career orientation, cultural enhancement, communication and technical skills, improved attendance, consumer awareness, and employment opportunity.

This year in the Shaw Community School, which holds classes several nights a week, the volunteer coordinator and the community school assistant principal are implementing the tutorial program, Operation Outreach, with the goal of increasing achievement levels of each participant by 4 months. Evidence will be documented by the SORT (Slosson Oral Reading Test) and a standardized math test. Volunteers also teach cooking, sewing, and crafts in the community school.

Dunbar Senior High School is a Washington institution; now housed in a new building, the "old Dunbar" graduated many black national leaders, particularly in the arts. Because of its location, Dunbar does not have access to many businesses but relies a great deal on the numerous black churches in the area as a source of volunteers. Like most D.C. schools, all of its students are black, and black pride messages are conspicuous in display cases and posters. The atmosphere of the school is quiet and controlled, but relationships between staff and students are apparently warm. At the time of our visit, the principal was on her way to a hospital to visit a student who had been injured in a car accident on the way to school.

The principal introduced us to the new president of the school's PTA, who was in the school as a volunteer. He is a black male librarian who meets weekly with English classes. Committee members also talked with a team of black professionals from one of the churches, which has started a mentoring and counseling program. The principal made clear that volunteers from churches understand that they may not use volunteering as a way of delivering religious messages. A volunteer schedule for the day showed the department and teacher with whom a volunteer was working and the volunteer's name and affiliation.

The D.C. public schools hosted a volunteer experiment in 1986–1988, in which a local civic group recruited mathematicians, scientists, and engineers from the entire metropolitan area to supplement and enhance the teaching of math and science in junior high schools. The project found that it was possible to attract professional people to schools in all neighborhoods of the city; a major stumbling block turned out to be uncertainty on the part of many teachers about how to use or react with another adult, who often has a Ph.D. degree, in their classrooms. Intensive training for teachers in which they were encouraged to write job descriptions for prospective volunteers led to better matches between volunteers and teachers; the program is continuing under an advisory committee of community representatives.

SUMMARY

In reviewing the committee's 13 site visits, the major impression shared by the members is that the impact of these volunteer programs on students was positive. This finding is not surprising in light of the fact that the sites were chosen because knowledgeable groups thought them to have exemplary volunteer programs.

It was evident from interviews that the programs were based on needs expressed by teachers at the participating schools. The programs came across as well organized and supported at the policy level. The committee was also impressed with the efforts in large cities and suburban areas where small staffs were able to deliver the services of thousands of volunteers to large numbers of schools and students. Despite these efforts, however, many of the volunteer coordinators interviewed expressed the view that there were many more students who could benefit from volunteer help than were receiving it and that greater efforts are needed.

Impressions of committee members were that those responsible for organizing and administrating these programs were able, caring, and committed people trying to help overburdened education systems meet the needs of students and that the programs were achieving positive results. But the committee found little in the way of formal evaluation studies to substantiate this positive view. Evaluations available even in these "exemplary" programs were largely informal attempts to determine teacher, administrator, or volunteer perceptions as to the value of the effort. For the most part, these "evaluations" are used by the administrators to monitor the program; they were particularly useful, the committee was told, in identifying problems that needed attention or in calling attention to particularly successful activities.

Those few studies that were directed to evaluating outcomes resulting from the use of volunteers were usually tied to projects carried out with outside funding from foundations or corporations, and they had an evaluation built into the project. These included, for example, a few studies measuring the effects of volunteer tutoring, which showed positive results. But even most of these evaluations were formalized attempts to get at perceptions of outcomes. Cost factors and conceptual problems, such as isolating variables or determining suitable measures of success, were among those cited by volunteer coordinators as obstacles to formal evaluation. For the most part, therefore, the committee had to rely on the available perception studies, informal evaluations, anecdotal information obtained in interviews, and their own observations and experience in assessing the value of the volunteer programs that were visited.

In general, the committee notes that although all of the volunteer coordinators were proud of their accomplishments, none pretended that these were any panacea for education or indeed anything more than some help for the process. It was pointed out that most of the tasks undertaken by volunteers could be handled by paid staff, but funds for such staff are not available, and without volunteer help the tasks would not be done. There simply is not enough money in any of the school systems to pay for the services that volunteers provide. Moreover, there are some services, usually involving enrichment, that could not be performed by school staff, such as lectures, presentations, or demonstrations by scientists, jurists, artists, and others with special expertise.

As part of their site visits, committee members asked volunteer administrators and others to give us their perceptions of impediments to their programs and to tell us how they dealt with them. Discussed were a range of problems, including: overcoming difficulties in recruiting sufficient numbers of volunteers; dealing with lack of commitment on the part of some volunteers or lack of knowledge as to how to use volunteer time effectively on the part of some teachers; and adapting to commitment changes at the policy level when school superintendents or school boards change. Some of these are factors that can inhibit the overall success of volunteer programs, which are discussed in more detail in the next chapter. However, the committee was told that when problems arise that affect students, such as volunteers who do not show up as agreed or are unable to work with a student, they are addressed immediately.

In its deliberations, the committee tried to view the volunteer contribution in perspective in order to assess its limitations as well as its potential. Volunteers usually spend 3 to 4 hours per week in a school. In the organized programs that were visited, volunteers are screened, oriented, provided training as appropriate, and assigned to work under the supervision of professional staff. All of the program coordinators noted that volunteer help is provided only to teachers who ask for it. Teachers who are skeptical of the value of volunteers or prefer not to have an additional person working with them in the classroom simply do not participate.

It was evident that no matter how effective a volunteer activity, it is only supplementary to a well-run education program. Although there is agreement that volunteer help can make a difference, neither school administrators nor the volunteer coordinators believe that any massive infusion of volunteers could make up the shortcomings of an underfunded, poorly run education system.

The committee also observes that volunteering is clearly a growing social movement. The volunteers we talked with said they feel good about their volunteer service. The programs seen all had policy-level support and considerable citizen participation, and there was excitement about what the volunteer programs have accomplished and their potential. In summary, the committee viewed the weight of evidence as to accomplishments of the volunteer programs it visited to be positive.

6

Factors in School Volunteerism

To examine and describe the factors that foster or inhibit successful school volunteer programs, the committee used information gained from the review of the literature and the site visits to exemplary programs as well as the individual knowledge and experience of its members.

The committee's study of school volunteers in the United States comes at a time when volunteer programs are becoming institutionalized in many school systems. That is, a school system has decided that the volunteer contribution is worthwhile and that to facilitate the use of volunteers someone has to be assigned responsibility for organizing, administering, and coordinating their activities. For convenience, the committee refers to such programs as organized programs. Its purpose is to distinguish these programs from the thousands of informal teacher-volunteer arrangements in which a teacher asks a parent for occasional assistance with some activity or a parent suggests that he or she would be willing to help. Thousands of such informal arrangements exist, and we must assume that they usually work well or are quickly terminated. Committee members did talk with a few teachers who had made such arrangements, but the members were not able to identify and study many of them. In its review and report on those factors that foster or inhibit volunteer programs, the committee focused its attention on organized volunteer programs.

CHARACTERISTICS OF SUCCESSFUL PROGRAMS

The committee notes that the structure and operation of successful programs are varied. Recruiting, support, and recognition of volunteers take various forms. Administrative arrangements can differ, although a district coordinator and staff generally take major responsibility for over-all volunteer activities, including record-keeping and preparation of re-cruiting and training materials, with the aid of a coordinator, often a volunteer, at each school. The school coordinator may be active in re-cruiting parents and neighborhood volunteers and may be responsible for orienting, training, and placing volunteers in that building, as well as collecting and forwarding data on hours worked and services performed and working with teachers to evaluate the program. In some instances, programs are administered by a nonprofit organization working closely with the school district; there are a few instances (as described in Chapter 5) in which programs are administered by the volunteers themselves.

Support by Top Policy Levels

Strong support at the top policy and administrative levels in a school system is one of the major characteristics of a successful school volunteer program. In many cases, support for volunteers in schools is expressed in writing or regulations by the school board; a number of volunteer admin-istrators said they believe that such a board position, publicly announced, is essential. Beyond this, sincere personal acceptance and approval by the district board of education, the superintendent, and each participating school principal is apparent in successful programs. The committee also notes that teachers are more likely to welcome and use volunteers when the principal's support is clear and enthusiastic.

State-level support, in the few states where it exists, also seems to help greatly. A person or office in the state education agency assigned respon-sibility for promoting the use of volunteers, plus some state funding to local education agencies for that purpose, encourages school districts to participate. In general, states lag behind their local school systems in recognizing the potential contribution of volunteers.

Organization and Management

Sound organization and management are a major characteristic of suc-cessful school volunteer programs. Most of the volunteer programs the committee visited are districtwide operations managed by a director or coordinator of volunteer services (titles and specific duties varied) who was a school district employee. In a few instances, highly successful volunteer programs are operated by nonprofit organizations partly sup-ported by and working closely with a school district, and there were also programs that had been organized and were still managed by volunteers.

All of the districtwide programs reviewed by the committee had some form of centralized administrative structure. Most operate under written policy statements; all have generalized goals; and most have practical program objectives. In these programs, the district director of volunteer services works to involve as many schools as possible in the use of volunteers.

In most cases, the coordinator or a district staff member works with teachers and administrators in each school to assess the school's need for volunteers. The central volunteer office then either recruits and places volunteers directly, as a service to the schools, or trains a school team (usually consisting of a volunteer and a member of the staff) to conduct recruiting and to orient and train the school's volunteers. In well-established programs, needs assessment is not a one-time event; ongoing reassessment at each school allows the coordinator to shift and redirect volunteer resources as needs change.

The district volunteer coordinator usually develops procedures to be followed by the schools in managing their volunteer programs. The committee was impressed with the quality of many of the manuals, record-keeping forms, recognition programs, and public relations materials developed by volunteer offices. As has been noted above, the major administrative deficiencies are in data collection and evaluation, which are weak even in exemplary programs. The district volunteer coordinator is often responsible for cultivating community or business contacts, and effective coordinators appeared to spend considerable time trouble-shooting and problem-solving with school staff, volunteers, and business and community partners.

A significant characteristic of all of the volunteer programs the committee examined is the energy, creativity, and efficiency with which they are administered. In most instances, very small staffs seem to accomplish near miracles in dealing with paperwork and the many personal contacts involved in volunteer programs. Many school volunteer programs are quite young, and some are still headed by the individuals who created them 10 or so years ago. Others headed by successors to the program originators continue to expand the services and to introduce new aspects to volunteerism. It is worth noting that a new group of administrators of business-school partnerships is now emerging, with some broadened responsibilities that often include many kinds of business involvement in education, in addition to placing volunteers in schools. These activities—which may include material gifts of equipment, work opportunities for teachers or students, and other relationships—were considered beyond the scope of this study.

Most existing volunteer programs came to their present administrative effectiveness by trial and error over a period of years. The experiences of those early programs are reflected in training materials now available, through the national school volunteer association (National Association of

Partners in Education) and some state volunteer offices, that aid schools or districts in developing programs responsive to their particular local needs and resources. Volunteer program coordinators now have access to planning guides and training materials to help them organize and manage volunteer programs.

Involvement of Teachers

Another significant factor in successful school volunteer programs appears to be the relationships between volunteer coordinators and teachers. Many volunteer activities require close cooperation between a volunteer and a teacher. Successful volunteer programs try to deal with the issue of teacher participation by providing orientation to the objectives and potential of a volunteer program, not only for volunteers but also for teachers and other school staff. Almost all volunteer programs find that some teachers are pleased to work with volunteers, but others are unwilling, either from timidity and concern about being observed by outsiders or as a matter of educational philosophy. As a basic principle, most programs place volunteers only with teachers who request them and make clear that volunteers work only under the supervision of teachers.

Some schools provide specific training to teachers, as well as to volunteers, in the techniques of cooperating and developing coordinated activities for students. Many of the teachers interviewed during the committee's site visits noted that they had received no training in the use of volunteers during their professional preparation and that training was very helpful in working effectively with volunteers.

The attitude of teacher unions toward the use of volunteers was of interest to the committee. Both of the major teacher organizations support the use of volunteers in schools, with the provision that they work under the supervision of professional teaching staff and are not used to replace teachers or school aides. During several of the site visits, union leaders indicated that their members welcome volunteers as a source of help that the school system could not otherwise afford. They saw no problem that volunteers might become an alternative to paid teacher aides. In one major urban school system, the policy of the board of education in support of school volunteers actually specifies that they may not be used to justify a reduction in force.

Recruitment, Training, and Placement of Volunteers

Successful school volunteer programs recruit volunteers from many sources: the PTA or PTO, the Junior League, the local RSVP (Retired Senior Volunteers Program), businesses, colleges and universities, sometimes elementary and secondary school students, and, always, parents. The programs consider the human resources available in their communities in determining recruiting strategies: in areas with large retirement populations, for example, the programs aim at recruiting senior citizens; those close to colleges or universities seek college students; and in some instances, contact has been made with nearby military bases.

As recently as a decade ago, most volunteers were parents, and most of these were parents of children in the school. This pattern is, of course, changing as many mothers are now employed and are unavailable to help during school hours. Programs reviewed by the committee indicate that they now spread a wide recruiting net, hoping to bring in not only retired senior citizens and college and high school students but also employees on released time from their jobs in business and industry. Recruiting is conducted in many ways: with brochures, posters, newspaper articles and advertisements, spot announcements on radio and television, and, very importantly, by word of mouth. The best recruiter, program coordinators say, is an enthusiastic volunteer.

Success in recruiting enough volunteers with the attributes requested by teachers is a constant challenge to volunteer program coordinators and requires constant effort. Most coordinators note that they usually had more requests than they could easily fill.

Once volunteers are recruited, virtually all organized programs provide orientation often in joint meetings with school staff, about the general nature of the undertaking on which they are embarking. For volunteers and staff, this orientation usually includes an introduction to the philosophy and objectives of the volunteer program and the needs the program will attempt to meet. For volunteers, orientation also usually includes a briefing on practical matters, such as the physical facilities of the school (is there a meeting or work room for volunteers, where can volunteers park, may they eat lunch at school?) and school rules and expectations, including the need to maintain confidentiality about student performance and records. Commitment by the volunteer is stressed; orientation sessions usually emphasize the importance of punctuality, and volunteers are asked to notify the school if they are unable to keep scheduled assignments. Most programs have also developed written guidelines for volunteers.

In programs that involve contact with students, particularly the one-on-one relationships of tutoring and mentoring, volunteers are often asked to commit to the activity for a specific period of time on a regular basis. Coordinators speak of the possible harm that can be done if a volunteer drops out of a student's life without cause or explanation, leaving the young person with a sense of failure and rejection.

In addition to basic orientation, many programs report that they also provide volunteers some form of specialized training, related to the work they will perform. Sometimes this training is provided by the teacher or staff person with whom the volunteer will be working. In other cases, the volunteer program staff or consultants may present seminars on such subjects as tutoring, reading, mathematics, working with handicapped youngsters, and listening to children. The amount of training volunteers received in programs reviewed by the committee varied considerably, depending on the task assigned. In some instances, it was intense and extended over a considerable time period. For the most part, however, training amounted to only a few hours per semester.

When volunteers are aiding elementary teachers by reading to children or occupying some of them in arts and crafts activities while the teacher works with others, only minimal training is considered necessary. As one teacher put it: "We need warm, caring people to listen to groups of children, perhaps read to them, or organize arts and crafts, to give us time to work with small groups and focus on whatever is needed." But a project that made extensive use of volunteers to improve thinking and writing skills provided extensive training through formally organized after-school workshops for both teachers and volunteers, with experts brought in to lecture and lead the workshops. The Junior Great Books program, a widely used volunteer program, requires that volunteers attend training sessions for a fee. Many coordinators believe that improvement in training would lead to even better results from volunteer efforts.

How volunteers are assigned to given activities or classrooms appears to vary widely. Most district-level coordinators place considerable reliance on school building volunteer coordinators to know the teachers, students, and volunteers well enough to make good matches. Volunteers are asked on application and registration forms to indicate their areas of special interest, and this serves as a general guide. Usually, the volunteer candidate is also interviewed.

Despite the best efforts, however, volunteers do not always work out in specific assignments. In such cases, coordinators say they use a variety of strategies to correct the problem and will reassign the volunteer if necessary. Some programs noted that uncertainty about what the volunteer is expected to do can produce problems; agreement between the teacher and the volunteers as to what they hope to accomplish and how to go about it helps to prevent misunderstandings.

Recognition of Volunteers

Successful programs give much time and attention to the way volunteers are treated. Retaining volunteers was high on most coordinators' agendas, and programs apparently exchange more information about recognition than any other single issue. It is common for a school system to sponsor some kind of gala social event near the end of the school year, to which all volunteers are invited. In addition, individual schools and teachers use a variety of techniques, including notes of appreciation, pins, plaques, bulletin board postings, and the like, to salute volunteers.

These practices are probably helpful in retaining volunteers. However, the committee heard from a number of volunteers, particularly corporate volunteers and professionals providing specialized services, that they would prefer recognition in the form of information from the schools about whether and how their volunteering makes a difference to students, specifically youngsters they have been tutoring or mentoring. In one case, volunteers declined to attend a recognition event that conflicted with their regularly scheduled activities with students.

FACTORS INHIBITING THE USE
OF VOLUNTEERS IN SCHOOLS

Much of the evidence for the committee's analysis of inhibiting factors was obtained from interviews, and the information was largely anecdotal. Nevertheless, the questions raised did provide some insights as to what prevents successful use of volunteers in schools. In general, the committee found that inhibiting factors can be grouped under two major categories: those that prevent volunteer programs from being established or, once established, from flourishing, and those factors that inhibit success in some aspect of an ongoing program.

In considering the first category, the committee attempted to determine why many schools have no volunteer programs. The data reported to the National Center for Education Statistics show that about 40 percent of schools surveyed reported no use of volunteers. Committee members attempted to identify a few such schools and to find out why, and they also questioned people with expertise in education. No definitive answers were possible given the time and constraints of this study, but the committee did gain some insight. Reasons for not using volunteers varied. In some instances, it was simply lack of awareness. In others, there was knowledge of the potential, but inertia, other priorities, and lack of know-how to go about getting started evidently accounted for no volunteer activity. Still other comments cited hostility to the use of volunteers by local teacher and teacher aide organizations. Even though the national organizations of these groups support the use of volunteers under stated conditions, some local groups continued to be suspicious.

The negative attitudes of school administrators were another reason: some school superintendents and some school principals still perceive volunteers as outside intruders and possible troublemakers. During the 1980s many school superintendents became receptive to community involvement as part of a public relations strategy to increase public support for education. But even in districts where superintendents gave open support to volunteerism as part of this strategy, support by principals varied from school to school, and some resisted using volunteers.

The committee was also told that many teachers declined to use volunteers for various reasons. Some teachers view volunteers as someone looking over their shoulder and watching their performance, and they do not want to be scrutinized; they do not want what they perceive as interference from outsiders. Some teachers perceive volunteers as possible gossips and "butt-ins." Others consider the time spent in training someone who would be coming in twice a week for a few hours too high a price to pay for the help that could be received. Still others saw conflict with their teaching style or felt strongly that education should be provided by trained educators and were philosophically opposed to bringing noneducators into the classroom. There was speculation that the training that educators receive in college usually does not prepare them to use outside resources. The contention is that teachers who have not had training in supervision of volunteer help worry about how to use volunteers or are sometimes reluctant to take on what they perceive as a burden rather than a help. Volunteer coordinators, many of whom supplied some of the above anecdotes, noted that they do not try to impose volunteers on reluctant teachers. Instead they work in a school with those teachers who do want help.

In attempting to understand the factors that inhibit success or even result in failure of volunteer programs after they are initiated, the committee found that they are often simply the reverse of the factors identified as essential for successful programs: poor coordination or sloppy management, lack of adequate orientation and screening, and confusion over objectives are among factors frequently cited. From volunteers, there were stories that the teacher they were assigned to work with did not know how to make good use of their time. Teachers have many complaints that volunteers do not always know what is expected of them or that they have insufficient commitment and fail to show up as planned. Such complaints, according to volunteer coordinators, can usually be traced to inadequate screening and orientation, poor coordination, insufficient training, or, occasionally, even personality differences. Good managers, committee members were told, try to anticipate such problems before they arise and deal with them quickly when they do.

Inadequate assessment of the time and commitment required to accomplish objectives was another illustration of a factor that can severely inhibit the effectiveness of a program. Activities such as tutoring, which take place over a period of time, require considerable planning and a clear understanding of what is required if they are to show success.

Confusion or mismatch of objectives can also result in program failure. One illustration given was of an offer by the corporate officers of a television station to adopt a school. The volunteer coordinator saw this as an opporunity for a school to work with a glamorous organization, one that could interest and motivate students. What was not perceived, however, were the differences in objectives. The school administrators and teachers wanted a sharing of expertise in the curricular sense, with station volunteers serving as mentors, providing career guidance, motivating students, and sharing their knowledge in what many perceive as a glamorous field. But the corporate officers of the station perceived the relationship in a very different way: they were interested in establishing good public relations with the community and saw this in a promotional sense. They offered tickets to concerts and other events, T-shirts, materials, and even an occasional speaker; they were not thinking in terms of releasing station staff to work with students in the school or to bringing students to the station on a regular basis. The result was disappointment on both sides. The volunteer coordinator who described this problem assumed the blame for not recognizing the conflicting objectives. As a result of this experience, such business-school relationships are now planned more carefully in this district.

Probably the most important of inhibiting factors is loss of support at the top policy or administrative level. Since volunteer programs are usually not mandated by states, they may be dispensed with or cut back at the discretion of a superintendent or school board. Thus, when a change occurs in school superintendents or in school boards, volunteer administrators must often justify their activity and persuade others of its value. Because most volunteer programs have very small staffs, any cutback can severely inhibit a program.

OBSERVATIONS ON NATIONAL VOLUNTARY YOUTH SERVICE

During the course of the committee's study of school volunteers, the U.S. Congress became actively involved in introducing and debating legislation to set up some kind of voluntary national service for young people, in some instances providing for incentives such as stipends for service. A major component of the proposed legislation would be volunteer service in community agencies and organizations. Such an approach could make large numbers of additional volunteers available to schools.

From its study of school volunteers, the committee can make some suggestions about voluntary youth service that may be helpful in the debate. Following the site visits by committee members to the exemplary programs, follow-up contact was made with the volunteer administrators and with others to ask their views as to the possible effects on their programs of national service legislation.

Virtually all volunteer administrators or coordinators told us that to be successful, national voluntary youth service programs would require an administrative infrastructure at the local level to assess the needs of schools and classrooms, to match volunteer skills and interests to needs, to monitor volunteer activities, to address issues such as liability and insurance, and to maintain records and evaluate the effects of the program. They considered it most important that local agencies be able to provide thorough orientation and guidance and ensure appropriate supervision of volunteers, especially those in activities involved with the instructional process and dealing directly with students, such as tutoring or mentoring. These latter activities and some others often require training as well as orientation, and volunteers may be ineffective without it, particularly since those volunteering as a result of the legislation are likely to be young persons, many of whom have just finished high school.

Virtually all of those interviewed said that their agencies could absorb and effectively use additional volunteer help, but most said they would need funds for additional staff to handle them effectively. It was pointed out, however, that Congress should be aware of the many areas in the country that do not have organized volunteer programs and where no local administrative infrastructure exists.

The likelihood that persons volunteering as a result of national service legislation would be available on a full-time basis was considered another challenge. As already noted, most volunteers provide part-time help, usually only 3 to 4 hours, 2 to 3 days a week. How to use full-time volunteers effectively is a question that would have to be addressed. Moreover, availability of such full-time service may raise objections from teacher aides organizations, which are likely to view such volunteers as possible substitutes for full-time staff.

The committee urges Congress to consider such issues in connection with any voluntary youth service legislation.

CONCLUSIONS AND RECOMMENDATIONS

As a result of its examination of school volunteer programs, the committee has concluded that volunteers do make significant contributions to education and that schools have need of and could not otherwise afford many of the services volunteers can provide. The committee believes equally strongly, however, that volunteer activities should be thoughtfully planned, organized, and focused. The committee therefore makes two recommendations:

- The committee recommends that educators, school boards, community leaders, and state and federal public officials become informed about and support the development of school volunteer programs.

- The committee recommends that volunteer programs be designed to complement and support the educational objectives of schools.

7

A Call to Action

The whole people must take upon themselves
the education of the whole people.

President John Adams

This study on the use of volunteers in the public schools is the product of the interest of the Congress and the concerns of the U.S. Department of Education. Mandated by Congress and supported by the department, it is the first comprehensive attempt to provide scope and understanding to the phenomenon of school volunteerism.

The committee spent 18 months studying the issues. Members have talked with and listened to experts at all levels, including those who run the school systems, those responsible for volunteer programs, the teachers and other school personnel who make use of the services and direct the activities of the volunteers, the volunteers themselves, and the students and others who are the beneficiaries. We have listened to academics as well as policy makers at the federal and state levels, explored the literature, and traveled widely. Throughout, each of us has brought to the task his or her respective and unique expertise that, taken together, has enabled us to see the broad canvas of our efforts.

CONCLUSIONS

We believe that the school volunteer movement is a serious response to serious educational problems that face the nation today and for some time to come. In the course of its study, the committee has come to admire and appreciate the efforts and manifold contributions that volunteers make on behalf of students across America.

Volunteerism constitutes a resource of potentially huge dimensions, one that has barely been tapped and that can help schools better respond to many disturbing changes in our society—the greater fragility of family life, the damaging danger of drugs, and the widening gap between the privileged and the deprived. Volunteers provide benefits to schools that otherwise would be unavailable. School volunteers truly represent what President Bush has called "a thousand points of light."

The committee wishes to emphasize most strongly, however, that the use of volunteers in schools is not and cannot be a substitute for public funding of education. Nor should it allow any violation of the principle of professionalism through the substitution of volunteers for professionally trained educators. Volunteers are a supplemental resource, reflecting the complex interaction of individual and local initiatives that draw on local experience, leadership, and management. In the same vein, the committee cautions against dependence on individuals and corporate philanthropy to provide comprehensive educational goods and services.

The committee concludes that much remains to be done if the great resource of volunteers is to be understood and used to its fullest potential. Although it found some research studies, ample anecdotal evidence, and many informal evaluations of the value of volunteer service, much more scholarly, empirical research on the effects of volunteers on school staff, student motivation, and performance is needed. Simply put, the educational community needs better research and evaluation on the effects of school volunteer programs. It needs more information better disseminated about what determines the success of both small and large programs, what is needed, and what works best.

The committee also urges school systems that expand their volunteer programs to try to ensure some balance in the distribution of volunteer resources among schools in affluent and in poor areas. Expansion could carry unintended and potentially negative consequences if the result is greater inequity between rich and poor schools. It is important to consider whether the introduction of incentives such as stipends may adversely effect the motivation, effectiveness, and representativeness of the volunteer pool. In all these instances, policy makers as well as administrators and teachers must be sensitive to the possibility of unintended consequences.

The committee emphasizes the need for adequate statistics on the use of school volunteers. Our efforts to document changes in the size of the volunteer group over time and to profile its characteristics were hampered by insufficient reliable and consistent national data.

The committee became aware, during its deliberations, of the growing interest in national service programs, as exemplified by the different legislative initiatives proposed in 1989. Although our charge did not extend to an in-depth review of this issue or of the individual legislative proposals, the subject did arise frequently in conversations with local officials during our visits to observe the different volunteer programs. Those interactions, coupled with our interest in these programs as sources of supply of volunteers, and when added to the expertise present within the committee, have led us to several observations concerning the implementation of a national service program as a source of school volunteers.

The issues that require understanding and agreement on the part of authorities at all levels include ensuring that the program not overwhelm the local capability, that the volunteers can be used efficiently and effectively, and that adequate supervisory capability exists. The number and type of volunteers should be determined by the local authority, and it is advisable that any stipends be commensurate with performance. Adequate training should be provided to volunteers so that they understand their roles vis à vis the local educational establishment. Finally, research and evaluation to measure the effects should be integral components of any program. Above all, the federal role should be one of assistance—providing guidelines, carrying out research, disseminating information, and acting as a clearinghouse; carrying out the program must be left to local leadership.

RECOMMENDATIONS

Although we are fully aware and supportive of the fact that the key responsibility for developing and implementing programs that use volunteers lies with local leadership, we are nonetheless equally of the belief that thoughtful and reasoned national policy can substantially assist in nourishing the creativity of volunteer programs in thousands of schools and districts.

Accordingly, we strongly recommend that to accomplish these objectives:

- The President use his good offices to encourage and support the school volunteer movement;
- The Secretary of Education exercise leadership by
  —establishing an office in the department to encourage promotion by the states of local volunteer activities, to help states coordinate such efforts through dissemination of information, and to encourage private sector volunteer activities;
  —supporting research and evaluation studies on the processes and the consequences of the use of volunteers in schools; and
  —taking responsibility for the collection, analysis, and dissemination of national data on the use of volunteers in schools; and
- The Congress provide funds to states to enable them to encourage and organize local school volunteer activities, provide support for the activities proposed by the President and those to be under-

taken by the U.S. Department of Education, and provide a forum for the stimulation of ideas to further the objectives of volunteerism in the public schools.

More specific recommendations with respect to data collection; research and evaluation; and participation by educators, school boards, community leaders, and state and federal officials are presented at the end of Chapters 3, 4, and 6.

Appendix A

Data from NCES Schools and Staffing Survey, 1987–1988

The data shown in the tables in Appendix A are derived from the 1987–1988 School and Staffing Survey, conducted by the National Center for Education Statistics (NCES). The data are both preliminary and unpublished and are the product of special tabulations prepared for the committee by NCES. When final results of the survey are published by NCES, they undoubtedly will reflect corrections as well as adjustments for nonreponse, both to the survey and to a specific question within the survey content. For these reasons, slight differences may be expected in the final published results.

The totals shown in the following tables reflect a simple ratio adjustment for all types of nonresponse; the detail, however, has not been adjusted for any of the possible causes of nonresponse. Accordingly, the detail does not add to the total and differs somewhat among the tables. Because of rounding, both for the numbers and the percentage distribution, the detail may not add exactly to the total.

NA/NR denotes that the data are not available or were not reported.

TABLE A-1 Public Schools with Unpaid Volunteers, by Enrollment Size

Enrollment	Schools Total	No Volunteers	With Volunteers	Volunteers per School 1–5	6–20	20+
NUMBER						
Total	78,714	31,412	47,302	17,044	17,860	12,397
Less than 150	7,255	4,247	3,008	1,817	1,089	103
150–299	12,727	5,569	7,158	3,539	2,693	927
300–499	21,503	7,350	14,153	4,641	5,743	3,769
500–749	16,219	5,404	10,815	2,834	3,940	4,042
More than 750	12,801	5,648	7,153	2,407	2,504	2,242
NA/NR	10,051					
PERCENT						
Total	100.0	40.0	60.0	21.6	22.7	15.7
Less than 150	100.0	58.5	41.5	25.0	15.0	1.4
150–299	100.0	43.8	56.2	27.8	21.2	7.3
300–499	100.0	34.2	65.8	21.6	26.7	17.5
500–749	100.0	33.3	66.7	17.5	24.3	24.9
More than 750	100.0	44.1	55.9	18.8	19.6	17.5

NOTE: See text at beginning of Appendix A.

TABLE A-2 Public Schools with Unpaid Volunteers, by Percent Minority Enrollment

Minority Enrollment	Schools Total	No Volunteers	With Volunteers	Volunteers per School 1–5	6–20	20+
NUMBER						
Total	78,714	31,412	47,302	17,044	17,860	12,397
Less than 5	25,178	11,346	13,832	5,315	5,515	3,002
5–19	16,610	5,779	10,831	3,185	3,799	3,846
20–49	13,054	4,780	8,274	2,730	3,060	2,485
50–74	6,480	2,384	4,096	1,637	1,554	904
More than 75	8,158	3,487	4,671	2,154	1,804	712
NA/NR	11,078					
PERCENT						
Total	100.0	40.0	60.0	21.6	22.7	15.7
Less than 5	100.0	45.1	54.9	21.1	21.9	11.9
5–19	100.0	34.8	65.2	19.2	22.9	23.2
20–49	100.0	36.6	63.4	20.9	23.4	19.0
50–74	100.0	36.8	63.2	25.3	24.0	14.0
More than 75	100.0	42.7	57.3	26.4	22.1	8.7

NOTE: See text at beginning of Appendix A.

TABLE A-7 Number of Private Schools with Unpaid Volunteers, by Enrollment Size

Enrollment	Schools Total	No Volunteers	With Volunteers	Volunteers per School 1–5	6–20	20+
NUMBER						
Total	27,126	9,388	17,738	8,854	5,458	3,427
Less than 150	10,178	4,192	5,986	4,120	1,537	329
150–299	6,091	1,470	4,621	1,897	1,600	1,124
300–499	2,564	697	1,867	484	710	673
500–749	1,022	258	764	209	237	318
More than 750	571	217	354	75	97	181
NA/NR	11,611					
PERCENT						
Total	100.0	34.6	65.4	32.6	20.1	12.6
Less than 150	100.0	41.2	58.8	40.5	15.1	3.2
150–299	100.0	24.1	75.9	31.1	26.3	18.5
300–499	100.0	27.2	72.8	18.9	27.7	26.3
500–749	100.0	25.3	74.7	20.4	23.2	31.1
More than 750	100.0	38.1	61.9	13.1	17.1	31.8

NOTE: See text at beginning of Appendix A.

TABLE A-8 Number of Private Schools with Unpaid Volunteers, by Percent Minority Enrollment

Minority Enrollment	Schools Total	No Volunteers	With Volunteers	Volunteers per School 1–5	6–20	20+
NUMBER						
Total	27,126	9,388	17,738	8,854	5,458	3,427
Less than 5	8,887	2,685	6,202	2,739	2,092	1,371
5–19	5,781	1,684	4,097	1,937	1,419	740
20–49	2,607	986	1,621	904	385	332
50–74	1,050	471	579	381	101	96
More than 75	1,819	899	920	747	115	58
NA/NR	11,893					
PERCENT						
Total	100.0	34.6	65.4	32.6	20.1	12.6
Less than 5	100.0	30.2	69.8	30.8	23.5	15.4
5–19	100.0	29.1	70.9	33.5	24.6	12.8
20–49	100.0	37.8	62.2	34.7	14.8	12.7
50–74	100.0	44.9	55.1	36.3	9.6	9.1
More than 75	100.0	49.4	50.6	41.0	6.3	3.2

NOTE: See text at beginning of Appendix A.

TABLE A-9   Number of Private Schools with Unpaid Volunteers, by Percent Minority Teachers

Minority Teachers	Schools			Volunteers per School		
	Total	No Volunteers	With Volunteers	1–5	6–20	20+
NUMBER						
Total	27,126	9,388	17,738	8,854	5,458	3,427
Less than 5	13,865	4,229	9,636	4,443	3,219	1,974
5–19	3,024	899	2,125	1,099	592	433
20–49	1,358	601	757	521	160	77
50–74	571	284	287	242	27	18
More than 75	679	459	220	162	24	34
NA/NR	12,540					
PERCENT						
Total	100.0	34.6	65.4	32.6	20.1	12.6
Less than 5	100.0	30.5	69.5	32.0	23.2	14.2
5–19	100.0	29.7	70.3	36.3	19.6	14.3
20–49	100.0	44.3	55.7	38.3	11.8	5.6
50–74	100.0	49.8	50.2	42.5	4.7	3.1
More than 75	100.0	67.6	32.4	23.8	3.6	5.0

NOTE: See text at beginning of Appendix A.

TABLE A-10   Number of Private Schools with Unpaid Volunteers, by Type of School

Type of School	Schools			Volunteers per School		
	Total	No Volunteers	With Volunteers	1–5	6–20	20+
NUMBER						
Total	27,126	9,388	17,738	8,854	5,458	3,427
Elementary	11,614	3,202	8,412	3,913	2,692	1,807
Middle/junior high	337	159	178	103	58	18
Secondary	1,757	932	825	394	210	221
Combined	4,014	1,630	2,384	1,460	596	328
Other	2,698	908	1,790	914	625	251
NA/NR	11,616					
PERCENT						
Total	100.0	34.6	65.4	32.6	20.1	12.6
Elementary	100.0	27.6	72.4	33.7	23.2	15.6
Middle/junior high	100.0	47.2	52.8	30.4	17.2	5.3
Secondary	100.0	53.0	47.0	22.4	12.0	12.6
Combined	100.0	40.6	58.4	36.4	14.8	8.2
Other	100.0	33.7	66.3	33.9	23.2	9.3

NOTE: See text at beginning of Appendix A.

TABLE A-11   Number of Private Schools with Unpaid Volunteers, by Type of Community

Type of Community	Schools Total	No Volunteers	With Volunteers	Volunteers per School 1–5	6–20	20+
NUMBER						
Total	27,126	9,388	17,738	8,854	5,458	3,427
Rural/farming	3,816	1,635	2,181	1,262	715	205
Town[a]	4,737	1,217	3,520	1,779	1,105	636
Suburban	3,888	1,135	2,753	1,122	881	751
Urban	7,924	2,826	5,098	2,589	1,481	1,028
Other	35	29	6	—	—	6
NA/NR	11,636					
PERCENT						
Total	100.0	34.6	65.4	32.6	20.1	12.6
Rural/farming	100.0	42.8	57.2	33.1	18.7	5.4
Town[a]	100.0	25.7	74.3	37.6	23.3	13.4
Suburban	100.0	29.2	70.8	28.9	22.7	19.3
Urban	100.0	35.7	64.3	32.7	18.7	13.0
Other	100.0	82.8	17.2	—	—	17.2

NOTE: See text at beginning of Appendix A.
[a]Less than 50,000 population.

TABLE A-12   Number of Private Schools with Unpaid Volunteers, by Region

Region	Schools Total	No Volunteers	With Volunteers	Volunteers per School 1–5	6–20	20+
NUMBER						
Total	27,126	9,388	17,738	8,854	5,458	3,427
North Central	6,802	1,657	5,145	2,389	1,804	953
Northeast	4,794	1,652	3,142	1,443	1,013	687
South	5,372	2,517	2,855	1,684	713	458
West	3,465	1,018	2,447	1,268	652	527
NA/NR	11,603					
PERCENT						
Total	100.0	34.6	65.4	32.6	20.1	12.6
North Central	100.0	24.4	75.6	35.1	26.5	14.0
Northeast	100.0	34.5	65.5	30.1	21.1	14.3
South	100.0	46.9	53.1	31.4	13.3	8.5
West	100.0	29.4	70.6	36.6	18.8	15.2

NOTE: See text at beginning of Appendix A.

TABLE A-13   Number of Private Schools with Unpaid Volunteers, by Religious Orientation

Religious Orientation	Schools Total	No Volunteers	With Volunteers	Volunteers per School 1–5	6–20	20+
NUMBER						
Total	27,126	9,388	17,738	8,854	5,458	3,427
Secular	3,526	2,098	1,428	845	368	215
Religious	16,857	4,737	12,120	5,912	3,796	2,411
NA/NR	11,655					
PERCENT						
Total	100.0	34.6	65.4	32.6	20.1	12.6
Secular	100.0	59.5	40.5	23.9	10.4	6.1
Religious	100.0	28.1	71.9	35.1	22.5	14.3

NOTE: See text at beginning of Appendix A.

TABLE A-14   Number of Unpaid Volunteers in Public Schools, by Enrollment Size

Enrollment	Volunteers	Volunteers per School 1–5	6–20	20+
NUMBER				
Total	1,015,442	50,955	214,759	749,731
Less than 150	21,659	4,691	11,825	5,144
150–299	84,368	10,699	31,146	42,523
300–499	281,418	14,910	72,286	194,222
500–749	329,952	8,360	47,438	274,154
More than 750	194,383	7,045	30,230	157,109
PERCENT				
Total	100.0	5.0	21.1	73.8
Less than 150	100.0	21.7	54.6	23.7
150–299	100.0	12.7	36.9	50.4
300–499	100.0	5.3	25.7	69.0
500–749	100.0	2.5	14.4	83.1
More than 750	100.0	3.6	15.6	80.8

NOTE: See text at beginning of Appendix A.

TABLE A-15   Number of Unpaid Volunteers in Public Schools, by Percent Minority Enrollment

Minority Enrollment	Volunteers	Volunteers per School		
		1–5	6–20	20+
NUMBER				
Total	1,015,442	50,955	214,759	749,731
Less than 5	254,425	15,822	65,481	173,122
5–19	299,843	9,496	47,259	243,088
20–49	199,674	8,167	38,441	153,066
50–74	72,187	5,140	18,619	48,429
More than 75	72,454	6,495	20,260	45,699
PERCENT				
Total	100.0	5.0	21.1	73.8
Less than 5	100.0	6.2	25.7	68.0
5–19	100.0	3.2	15.8	81.1
20–49	100.0	4.1	19.3	76.7
50–74	100.0	7.1	25.8	67.1
More than 75	100.0	9.0	28.0	63.1

NOTE: See text at beginning of Appendix A.

TABLE A-16   Number of Unpaid Volunteers in Public Schools, by Percent Minority Teachers

Minority Teachers	Volunteers	Volunteers per School		
		1–5	6–20	20+
NUMBER				
Total	1,015,442	50,955	214,759	749,731
Less than 5	404,287	22,893	94,225	287,170
5–19	284,684	9,898	50,979	223,806
20–49	129,458	6,926	25,554	96,979
50–74	35,703	2,949	8,243	24,511
More than 75	14,053	1,088	4,653	8,313
PERCENT				
Total	100.0	5.0	21.1	73.8
Less than 5	100.0	5.7	23.3	71.0
5–19	100.0	3.5	18.0	78.6
20–49	100.0	5.3	19.7	74.9
50–74	100.0	8.3	23.1	68.7
More than 75	100.0	7.7	33.1	59.2

NOTE: See text at beginning of Appendix A.

TABLE A-17   Number of Unpaid Volunteers in Public Schools, by Type of School

Type of School	Volunteers	Volunteers per School		
		1–5	6–20	20+
NUMBER				
Total	1,015,442	50,955	214,759	749,731
Elementary	739,144	29,073	150,199	559,871
Middle/junior high	71,668	6,993	17,994	46,682
Secondary	61,231	5,192	12,132	43,906
Combined	18,864	2,668	7,335	8,861
Other	21,180	1,834	5,158	14,188
PERCENT				
Total	100.0	5.0	21.1	73.8
Elementary	100.0	3.9	20.3	75.7
Middle/junior high	100.0	9.8	25.1	65.1
Secondary	100.0	8.5	19.8	71.7
Combined	100.0	14.1	38.9	47.0
Other	100.0	8.7	24.4	67.0

NOTE: See text at beginning of Appendix A.

TABLE A-18   Number of Unpaid Volunteers in Public Schools, by Type of Community

Type of Community	Volunteers	Volunteers per School		
		1–5	6–20	20+
NUMBER				
Total	1,015,442	50,955	214,759	749,731
Rural/farming	140,881	15,883	53,059	71,939
Town[a]	210,479	11,071	51,765	147,643
Suburban	270,323	6,175	36,623	227,526
Urban	285,462	11,963	49,669	223,830
Other	4,112	441	1,482	2,190
PERCENT				
Total	100.0	5.2	21.1	73.8
Rural/farming	100.0	11.3	37.7	51.0
Town[a]	100.0	5.3	24.6	70.1
Suburban	100.0	2.3	13.5	84.2
Urban	100.0	4.2	17.4	78.4
Other	100.0	10.7	36.0	53.3

NOTE: See text at beginning of Appendix A.
[a]Less than 50,000 population.

TABLE 19   Number of Unpaid Volunteers in Public Schools, by Region

Region	Volunteers	Volunteers per School		
		1–5	6–20	20+
NUMBER				
Total	1,015,442	50,955	214,759	749,731
North Central	194,618	13,843	52,883	127,892
Northeast	104,661	7,329	29,955	67,376
South	341,641	15,153	65,219	261,270
West	271,287	9,449	44,867	216,971
PERCENT				
Total	100.0	5.0	21.1	73.8
North Central	100.0	7.1	27.2	65.7
Northeast	100.0	7.0	28.6	64.4
South	100.0	4.4	19.0	76.5
West	100.0	3.5	16.5	80.0

NOTE: See text at beginning of Appendix A.

TABLE A-20   Number of Unpaid Volunteers in Private Schools, by Enrollment Size

Enrollment	Volunteers	Volunteers per School		
		1–5	6–20	20+
NUMBER				
Total	345,994	28,785	76,687	240,523
Less than 150	43,714	11,057	17,045	15,611
150–299	87,289	5,729	20,271	61,289
300–499	54,525	1,508	9,290	43,727
500–749	27,117	645	3,110	23,362
More than 750	17,564	213	1,308	16,044
PERCENT				
Total	100.0	8.3	22.2	69.5
Less than 150	100.0	25.3	39.0	35.7
150–299	100.0	6.6	23.2	70.2
300–499	100.0	2.8	17.0	80.2
500–749	100.0	2.4	11.5	86.2
More than 750	100.0	1.2	7.4	91.3

NOTE: See text at beginning of Appendix A.

TABLE A-21 Number of Unpaid Volunteers in Private Schools, by Percent Minority Enrollment

Minority Enrollment	Volunteers	Volunteers per School		
		1–5	6–20	20+
NUMBER				
Total	345,994	28,785	76,687	240,523
Less than 5	115,143	8,493	25,653	80,997
5–19	61,877	5,475	16,915	39,486
20–49	27,829	2,224	4,795	20,810
50–74	14,698	921	1,273	12,504
More than 75	5,917	1,833	1,206	2,879
PERCENT				
Total	100.0	8.3	22.2	69.5
Less than 5	100.0	7.4	22.3	70.3
5–19	100.0	8.8	27.3	63.8
20–49	100.0	8.0	17.2	74.8
50–74	100.0	6.2	8.7	85.1
More than 75	100.0	31.0	20.4	48.7

NOTE: See text at beginning of Appendix A.

TABLE A-22 Number of Unpaid Volunteers in Private Schools, by Percent Minority Teachers

Minority Enrollment	Volunteers	Volunteers per School		
		1–5	6–20	20+
NUMBER				
Total	345,994	28,785	76,687	240,523
Less than 5	170,762	12,876	39,941	117,945
5–19	39,950	3,273	7,147	29,529
20–49	6,770	1,178	1,620	3,972
50–74	1,390	621	228	541
More than 75	1,622	369	278	975
PERCENT				
Total	100.0	8.3	22.2	69.5
Less than 5	100.0	7.5	23.4	69.1
5–19	100.0	8.2	17.9	73.9
20–49	100.0	17.4	23.9	58.7
50–74	100.0	44.7	16.4	38.9
More than 75	100.0	22.7	17.1	60.1

NOTE: See text at beginning of Appendix A.

TABLE A-23   Number of Unpaid Volunteers in Private Schools, by Type of School

Type of School	Volunteers	Volunteers per School		
		1–5	6–20	20+
NUMBER				
Total	345,994	28,785	76,687	240,523
Elementary	146,103	10,697	33,275	102,131
Middle/junior high	1,998	226	578	1,194
Secondary	23,727	1,048	2,665	20,013
Combined	35,423	4,463	6,777	24,183
Other	22,947	2,719	7,718	12,510
PERCENT				
Total	100.0	8.3	22.2	69.5
Elementary	100.0	7.3	22.8	69.9
Middle/junior high	100.0	11.3	28.9	59.8
Secondary	100.0	4.4	11.2	84.3
Combined	100.0	12.6	19.1	68.3
Other	100.0	11.9	33.6	54.5

NOTE: See text at beginning of Appendix A.

TABLE A-24   Number of Unpaid Volunteers in Private Schools, by Type of Community

Type of Community	Volunteers	Volunteers per School		
		1–5	6–20	20+
NUMBER				
Total	345,994	28,785	76,687	240,523
Rural/farming	22,373	3,475	8,473	10,425
Town[a]	51,132	5,316	12,873	32,942
Suburban	62,202	3,286	11,685	47,231
Urban	94,189	6,978	17,992	69,220
Other	214	—	—	214
PERCENT				
Total	100.0	8.3	22.2	69.5
Rural/farming	100.0	15.5	37.9	46.6
Town[a]	100.0	10.4	25.1	64.4
Suburban	100.0	5.3	18.8	76.0
Urban	100.0	7.4	19.1	73.5
Other	100.0	—	—	100.0

NOTE: See text at beginning of Appendix A.
[a]Less than 50,000 population.

TABLE A-25 Number of Unpaid Volunteers in Private Schools, by Region

Region	Volunteers	Volunteers per School		
		1–5	6–20	20+
NUMBER				
Total	345,994	28,785	76,687	240,523
North Central	79,239	7,110	21,384	50,745
Northeast	54,821	4,043	12,640	38,138
South	39,533	4,649	8,609	26,274
West	56,615	3,350	8,390	44,874
PERCENT				
Total	100.0	8.3	22.2	69.5
North Central	100.0	9.0	27.0	64.0
Northeast	100.0	7.4	23.1	69.6
South	100.0	11.8	21.8	66.5
West	100.0	5.9	14.8	79.3

NOTE: See text at beginning of Appendix A.

TABLE A-26 Number of Unpaid Volunteers in Private Schools, by Religious Orientation

Religious Orientation	Volunteers	Volunteers per School		
		1–5	6–20	20+
NUMBER				
Total	345,994	28,785	76,687	240,523
Secular	21,284	2,373	4,042	14,869
Religious	208,690	16,725	46,803	145,162
PERCENT				
Total	100.0	8.3	22.2	69.5
Secular	100.0	11.1	19.0	69.9
Religious	100.0	8.0	22.4	69.6

NOTE: See text at beginning of Appendix A.

Appendix B

Annotated Bibliography

Ainsworth, Ellen. Parent involvement in schools: a parent's view. *Thrust for Educational Leadership* 6(3):6–8. 1977.

The parent's perspective on school volunteer programs is presented by an education consultant with the League of Women Voters and a concerned parent. Ainsworth offers a rundown of likely problems as a helpful warning to those who might expect a volunteer program to run smoothly on goodwill alone. On the district level, administrators are apt to ignore the help that volunteers have given, may have difficulty choosing members of advisory committees, must arrange training programs, and may encounter frustrations in the course of long-term projects. On the classroom level, teachers must learn to treat parents as coworkers, not rivals, and a coordinator must match volunteers' skills and personalities with needs. She offers suggestions and is convinced that parent volunteer programs do work, resulting in less alienation between the schools and the community.

American Association of School Administrators (AASA). *Citizens and the Schools: Partners in Education.* Arlington, Va.: AASA. 1984.

This booklet offers suggestions for citizens to become partners in education. It instructs them on how to get informed and involved. Those with a variety of skills and experiences may become volunteers and work in classrooms offering special help to children and assistance to teachers. Volunteers can also help children who have special needs. Citizens can participate in school board meetings by serving on task forces, joining the parent/community organization, and getting other organizations involved.

Citizens can also speak up about concerns, including budget issues, remembering that quality education may depend on their understanding and support.

Arkell, R. N. Are student helpers helped? *Psychology in the Schools* 12(1):113–115. 1975.

Using a nonequivalent control group design, the study found the three student-helper roles of tutor, clerical worker, and audiovisual operator ineffective in changing students' self-esteem, attitude toward school, performance in spelling, and achievement in arithmetic.

Armstrong, Patricia M., Cherise Northcutt, and Patrick Davis. Year End Evaluation Reports, Project Years 1985–1986 and 1986–1987, Project Book Your Time. San Francisco School Volunteers, San Francisco Unified School District, San Francisco, Calif.

The report evaluates student achievement as measured by the California Test of Basic Skills given by the San Francisco Unified School District. It also reviews questionnaires administered to teachers, students, and volunteers in an immigrant literacy project in which volunteers supplemented classroom activities by reading and listening to students. Some reading tutors were 5th grade students; others were adults. Test score data showed students in a school where the literacy project was implemented schoolwide (grades K–5) achieved greater gains in reading and language arts than students in a school in which only a few teachers participated. Both schools scored higher than control schools that did not have the program. Questionnaires showed positive reactions to the program by teachers and volunteers.

Armstrong, Patricia M., Patrick Davis, and Cherise Northcutt. Final Evaluation Report, Project Year 1986–1987, Project Interconnections II. San Francisco School Volunteers, San Francisco Unified School District, San Francisco, Calif.

An independent evaluation of a program designed to increase a group of high school students' oral proficiency in a foreign language by using volunteer college students to lead students in conversation found that the high school students were more confident and fluent in the foreign language at the end of the program and the college students were more likely to enter a career of foreign-language teaching.

Armstrong, Patricia M.. *Final Evaluation Report, Project Focus.* San Francisco, Calif.: San Francisco Unified School District. 1985.

The evaluation measured the quality and effectiveness of workshop presentations to volunteers, growth in volunteers' knowledge about learning disabilities and tutoring techniques, and growth in students' basic skills. Techniques included subjective workshop feedback and pre- and posttest scores of knowledge.

Armstrong, Patricia M., and Amy Bassell Crowe. *Final Evaluation Report, Project Math in Action.* San Francisco, Calif.: San Francisco Unified School District. 1988.

An evaluation of a 3-year demonstration project using volunteer teacher college students to help teachers implement cooperative learning and use of manipulatives in mathematics. Improvements were seen in student problem-solving performance and attitudes toward mathematics.

Armstrong, Patricia M., and Mary Jane Sims. *Final Evaluation Report, Project Year 1987–1988, Project Think/Write.* San Francisco, Calif.: San Francisco Unified School District. 1988.

Teachers and volunteers from business attended workshops taught by the Bay Area Writing Project. Business volunteers then went into classrooms to help improve critical thinking and writing skills of middle and high school students as preparation for future employment. Data found positive impacts on students, volunteers, and teachers.

Asche, Jane A. *Handbook for Principals and Teachers: A Collaborative Approach to Effective Involvement of Business/Community Volunteers at the School Site.* Alexandria, Va.: National Association of Partners in Education. 1989.

This manual, developed under the joint sponsorship of the National Association of Partners in Education and the National Education Association, with cosponsorship by the American Federation of Teachers and the National Association of Elementary School Principals, is aimed at helping principals, teachers, and volunteers work together effectively in schools and classrooms.

Baker, Diane V. Effects of Different Volunteer/Tutee Combinations on the Reading and Mathematics Achievement and Self-Concept of Elementary Tutees. Unpublished doctoral dissertation. College of Education, University of Miami. 1974.

The researcher found that the reading and mathematics achievement of minority-group girls (black and Hispanic) was enhanced by assigning high school student volunteers of like race as tutors. On the other hand, white students achieved higher gains when tutored by adults (ages 22–60), as opposed to students (ages 15–21).

Banta, Trudy W., and Sandra S. Lawson. *Evaluation of the Lenoir City, Tennessee, Schools Retirement Power in Education Project, 1979–1980.* University of Tennessee, Knoxville, Bureau of Educational Research and Service. 1980.

One year after its inception a project was evaluated in which 14 volunteers were trained to use Laubach reading materials to tutor 4th and 7th graders. This report provides a general program and location description, a review of the literature on volunteer tutoring programs, a discussion of program objectives, and interpretation of the data. The findings indicate that tutoring did not effect significant differences between tutored and nontutored students in reading achievement, absenteeism from school, attitude toward school, or grades. However, the one-to-one relationship with an adult role model was found to have a favorable impact on student self-concept, especially at the 4th grade level.

Barth, Robert Conrad. Perceptions of Volunteers and Children Working in a Second Grade Language-Experience Reading Program. Unpublished doctoral dissertation. School of Education, Lehigh University. 1975.

A major objective of the study was to investigate perceptions of volunteers and children as to positive and negative critical incidents in a program of volunteers working with children in reading. No significant differences were found among positive or negative incidents reported by volunteers and children. Both perceived volunteer instructional activities as beneficial. The researcher concluded that the "critical incident technique" can be effectively used with young children.

Bartholemew Consolidated School Corporation. *School Volunteer Program Two-Year Evaluation Report.* Columbus, Ind.: Bartholemew Consolidated School Corporation. 1980.

This report evaluates a volunteer program established in the Bartholomew School Corporation. Areas identified for evaluation were (1) the fulfillment or achievement of program objectives; (2) measurable differences in the volunteers' attitudes toward the schooling process and parenting skills, as well as their self-concept development and locus of control; (3) general reactions and perceived impact of the program; (4) the effect of volunteer programs on student achievement; and (5) the cost-effectiveness of the program. Data were gathered from questionnaires and interviews. A copy of the questionnaire is included.

Bechtold, Warren Willard. The Effect of a Tutorial Relationship Between High School Student Volunteers and Peer-Aged Moderately Retarded Students Participating in Individually Prescribed Programs of Physical Activity. Unpublished doctoral dissertation. School of Education, Boston University. 1977.

Twelve high school student volunteers worked one on one with 14 peer-aged moderately retarded students in Newton South High School and Peabody Special Education School on prescribed physical activities. The moderately retarded students improved significantly in gross motor proficiency and physical performance. The high school student volunteer tutor was positively influenced, cognitively and affectively, by the tutorial experience.

Bernstein, Martha. Schools and volunteers. *Childhood Education* 59(2): 100–101. 1982.

Schools can work with organizations, businesses, and families to involve community volunteers in developing educational policy and fiscal resources and in providing classroom teaching activities.

Bloom, B. S. The search for methods of group instruction as effective as one-to-one tutoring. *Educational Leadership* 41(8):4–17. 1984.

This study found that with a trained tutor 98 percent of students academically outperform those who are taught in conventional classrooms with 1 teacher to 30 students.

Brock, Henry C., III. *Parent Volunteer Programs in Early Childhood Education.* Hamden, Conn.: Shoe String Press. 1976.

This book was written, according to Brock, "to provide a practical resource for parents, teachers, librarians, and administrators—for all now involved, or considering becoming involved, in a parent volunteer program." There are chapters and subchapters on the need for parent volunteers, financial considerations, parent volunteer program designs, program goals and objectives, screening and placement of volunteers and recognition of their service, and evaluation of program objectives.

Carney, John M., Judith E. Dobson, and Russell L. Dobson. Using senior citizen volunteers in the schools. *Journal of Humanistic Education and Development* 25(3):136–143. 1987.

A grandparents' program of senior citizen volunteers was designed to provide elementary school children access to caring, supportive senior citizens and to provide opportunities for older adults to engage in meaningful activities in a school setting. Results of a program evaluation support the value of the volunteer program for both children and adults.

Carter, Joan. Volunteers in public schools. *School Business Affairs* 48(10):16–17, 28–29. 1982.

The Volunteers in Public Schools program in Volusia County, Florida, has brought expertise from the community to the classrooms, enabled school districts to stretch their resources, and generated support for the schools. The ways in which the program recruits, trains, utilizes, and recognizes its volunteers are discussed.

Cherry, Charleen. Parents plant kindergarten . . . children blossom. *Momentum* 11(2):14–17. 1980.

Parent volunteers refurbished a vacant classroom to create a kindergarten and became involved as aides. The author discusses what motivates parents toward school volunteer work: concern for quality education, the need for work experience, and the friendships and personal satisfaction gained from volunteering.

Clark, Donald, and James Hughes. *Volunteerism in Special Education Through Industry-Education Cooperation.* Buffalo, N.Y.: National Academy for Industry-Education Cooperation. August 1986.

This report describes activities and products of a 3-year project to prepare private sector volunteers to become actively involved in special education through a networking system of industry-education partnerships. The project conducted workshops and produced a training package that includes a program development handbook and an instructor's guide. The handbook describes the principles, advantages, processes, and techniques for involving industry volunteers in special education. It includes seven program planning steps and implementation guidelines for management orientation, community and public relations, recruitment of volunteers, performance monitoring, recognition and appreciation, and program evaluation. The guide also includes such information as position titles of target workshop participants, draft letters and brochures, a suggested workshop agenda, and evaluation forms.

Cleveland, Linda Crawford. The Use of Community Volunteers in a Rural Secondary School Gifted and Talented Program. Unpublished doctoral dissertation. Florida State University. 1980.

Thirty-one community volunteers were used to field-test a model developed by the researcher in which members of the community served as adjunct instructional personnel for gifted and talented 12th grade students. Overall findings indicated the model could be implemented as a strategy for enriching the education of gifted and talented children in rural areas.

Cohen, Neal M. Volunteerism in education: translating spirit into state action. *Educational Horizons* 60(3):101–105. 1982.

Criteria for implementation of school volunteer programs include effective incentives, resources, and political and administrative feasibility. Alternatives for state action include maintaining current state policy, providing leadership by endorsement and mandate, and enacting legislation to provide incentives for volunteerism.

Cohen, Peter A., James A. Kulik, and Chen-Lin C. Kulik. Educational outcomes of tutoring: a meta-analysis of findings. *American Educational Research Journal* 19(2):237–248. 1982.

A meta-analysis of findings on the educational outcomes of tutoring found positive effects on academic outcomes from both structured and unstructured tutoring programs in which students tutored other students, but effects were stronger in structured programs.

Cone, Richard, and Judith Johnson. Volunteers in Education. Paper presented at annual meeting of the American Educational Research Association. New York City, April 1981.

The results of nine studies evaluating the effectiveness of volunteer programs in schools were reviewed in an effort to answer three questions: What is the value of volunteers to schools? Why do people volunteer to work in classrooms? What is the effect of volunteering on the volunteer? Volunteers were from a university and a corporation in the late 1970s. The review points up the need for research specifically addressing the motivations for and benefits of volunteer activities.

Cuninggim, Whitty. Citizen volunteers: a growing resource for teachers and students. *Teaching Exceptional Children* 12(3):108–112. 1980.

The author offers guidelines for utilizing volunteers in educating handicapped children. Several programs using volunteers are mentioned: the kindergarten screening project, listener program, primary classroom volunteers, and secondary school volunteers. The importance of teacher support is stressed. Steps for the teacher to follow for involving volunteers in the classroom are reviewed.

Cuninggim, Whitty, and Dorothy Mulligan. *Volunteers and Children with Special Needs.* Alexandria, Va.: National Association of Partners in Education. 1979.

This report includes case studies of progams that use volunteers to help educate handicapped children and provides guidance for volunteers who work with handicapped children.

Dade County Public Schools. *School Volunteer Development Project.* Miami, Fla.: Dade County Public Schools. 1975.

An evaluation of performance in reading and mathematics of students in grades 2–6 compares those assisted by volunteer tutors with unaided students. The evaluation found a mean gain in grade equivalent of 1.02 for tutored students in reading, while those without tutoring gained 0.038 grades. In mathematics, the tutored groups' mean gain was 81 percent of a grade level, compared with a decline of 6 percent for the untutored. Dade County's School Volunteer Development Project was validated for national distribution by the Joint Dissemination Review Panel of the U.S. Office of Education as a National Diffusion Network program in 1981.

Dade County Public Schools. *Evaluation of Training for Turnabout Volunteers.* Miami, Fla.: Dade County Public Schools. 1980.

This report on changes in reading and mathematics performance by students in grades 1–6 who were tutored by students in grades 7–9 compared the effects achieved by tutors who were given special training with those achieved by untrained tutors working under teacher supervision.

Dade County Public Schools. *Evaluation of Adopt-A-Grandparent Program.* Miami, Fla.: Dade County Public Schools. 1987.

An evaluation of the 1985–1986 Dade County Public Schools Adopt-A-Grandparent program showed that the program appeared to impact favorably on all participating students' self-concepts and at-risk students' attitudes toward the elderly. Some positive impact was noted in senior citizen participants, particularly with respect to their levels of depression, but these changes were not as consistently positive as were those noted for students.

Dolly, John P., and Patricia D. Page. The lack of parent participation in rural schools. *Research in Rural Education* 1(2):53–57. 1983.

Parents of rural students with low California Test of Basic Skills scores were provided with free training to serve as classroom volunteers. The study report notes that most parents refused to serve as volunteers, did not complete training, and refused to believe their children needed remediation because of conflicting grade reports.

Eberwein, Lowell, Lois Hirst, and Susan Magedanz. *An Annotated Bibliography on Volunteer Tutoring Programs.* Lexington: University of Kentucky. 1976.

The first section of this annotated bibliography is a selected review of research on the effects of volunteer tutoring. The second section reviews eight articles and books on training programs for tutors. Programs reviewed included peer, cross-age, and adult tutors.

Federal City Council. *Scientists in the Classroom: One School District's Experience with Science and Mathematics Volunteers in Elementary and Secondary Schools.* Washington, D.C.: Federal City Council. 1987.

Reports on a 2-year project funded by the Federal City Council to determine if scientists, engineers, and mathematicians, working or retired, could be recruited as volunteers to work in their disciplines in District of

Columbia schools. The report concluded that volunteers are available in a metropolitan area, but teachers must be trained to work with other professionals. The project included an evaluation of the effects of the volunteers on students' feelings about science and mathematics. The evaluation design is available.

Filipczak, James, Ann Lordeman, and Robert M. Friedman. Parental Involvement in the Schools: Towards What End? Paper presented at annual meeting of the American Educational Research Association, New York City. April 1977.

A comprehensive review of the literature on parental involvement casts a critical eye on the work done in four areas—volunteerism, parent-school communication, parent training, and policy making—and finds it generally lacking in rigor. The literature often neglects to describe the causal relationships between increased parental involvement and its results, leaving the links to be inferred. The methodologies do not allow for careful measurement, and there is a paucity of follow-up information. In the field of volunteerism, for example, the literature extolls the virtues of various projects and outlines many ways of utilizing community resources. But for all the apparent success of these programs, little attention has been paid to measuring the outcomes or to evaluating the effect of volunteer activities on students, parents, teachers, and administrators. With such significant gaps in scholarship, the authors cannot help but reserve judgment on the worth of volunteer programs; more than plaudits are needed to demonstrate the value of parental involvement in the schools. The study includes an eight-page bibliography.

Gordon, Ira. What Does Research Say About the Effects of Parent Involvement on Schooling? Paper prepared for annual meeting of the Association for Supervision and Curriculum Development. 1978. Summary taken from *The Evidence Continues to Grow; Parent Involvement Improves Student Achievement*, an annotated bibliography, Anne Henderson, ed., National Center for Citizens in Education, Columbia, Md. 1987.

Gordon, developer of the Follow Through program, reviews pertinent research on parent involvement, including the School Impact Model, which involves direct participation by parents in the schools, from volunteering to serving on governance councils. He found almost no research on the effects of the school impact model on student achievement, partially because it is much more difficult to study.

Gottesman, Ruth L., Frances M. Cerullo,and Ruth G. Nathan. *Helping the Child with Learning Disabilities: A School Volunteer's Guide.* New York: Albert Einstein College of Medicine, Yeshiva University. (In collaboration with the New York City School Volunteer Program, Inc.)

The manual explains the nature of learning disabilities and offers guidance to volunteers who work with learning disabled children.

Gray, Sandra T. Increase productivity with volunteers. *School Business Affairs* 50(2):18, 36. 1984.

Advantages of volunteer programs including school business partnerships are described. Among them are lower costs, improving productivity, increasing student achievement, and expanding community support. Hints for successful implementations are offered.

Halperin, Samuel, and Daniel W. Merenda. *Noble Allies: Volunteers in the Schools.* Washington, D.C.: Council for Basic Education. 1986.

The need for and benefits of school volunteer programs are examined. The authors discuss the kinds of help citizen volunteers can offer, maintain that volunteers mean better schools, suggest new missions and new roles for volunteers, and point out that the business community's greatest contribution will come through activities that support not one but all schools.

Ham, Wayne Albert. Effects of a Voluntary Tutor Program on Self-Esteem and Basic Skills Achievement in the Primary Grades of a Southern Rural School System. Unpublished doctoral dissertation. University of Florida. 1977.

The purpose of the study was to determine what effects, if any, volunteer tutors might have on primary students in terms of academic achievement and self-esteem and whether it was worth the time, finances, and manpower required of a small rural school district to set up a volunteer tutoring program. Ham concluded that volunteer tutoring in basic skills, such as that which took place during the study, affected achievement scores positively in the areas of curriculum addressed directly by the tutoring effort. Language arts and reading scores showed "significant gains," but mathematics was less affected. However, it was clear that "a modest expenditure of funds may bring to pass significant gains in vocabulary, reading comprehension, and language expression."

Hedges, Henry G. *Using Volunteers in Schools: Final Report.* Ontario Institute for Studies in Education, St. Catherines Niagara Center. Toronto, Canada: Ontario Department of Education. 1972.

The two main sections of this report describe the general model for the Volunteer Parental Involvement Program and provide program documentation. The model is accompanied by materials developed for its implementation in schools. The report includes an evaluation of volunteer use in three schools, an analysis of the findings, and a general and selected bibliography.

Hedin, Diane. Students as teachers: a tool for improving school climate and productivity. *Social Policy* 17(3):42–47. 1987.

The article describes current use of peer and cross-age teaching; expected benefits to tutees, tutors, teachers, and society; and research on educational outcomes. The author believes peer and cross-age tutoring is less widely used than it should be because of lack of awareness on the part of teachers and administrators of the power of such interventions or lack of information about how to organize programs.

Herzig, Shoshana. Junior high school students as teaching aides. *Arithmetic Teacher* 21(4):333–335. 1974.

The use of student aides to help implement and staff a mathematics laboratory is discussed. The actual types of help given are presented, as well as the effect the program had on the aides themselves as they were able to demonstrate acceptance of responsibility and gain self-confidence from the experience.

Hickey, Howard W. Community education's implications for teaching. *Journal of Teacher Education* 28(4):19–20. 1977.

Hickey notes a growing movement to break down the walls between the community and the classroom. "Volunteers can offer their expertise and experience, as well as their concern, and community activities can offer the most stimulating classroom of all." He suggests the major obstacle to community education is not logistics, finances, or politics but educators' attitudes. "They should continue to make the crucial decisions about the most rewarding environment for learning, but they must sometimes relinquish their podiums to the unacknowledged experts around us—the veteran next door, the musician across the street, or the service station owner down the block."

Hill, Corrine Paxman. A Comparative Study of Formal Volunteer Programs in Educational Settings. Unpublished doctoral dissertation. Department of Educational Administration, University of Utah. 1980.

Data were collected from 58 school volunteer programs and 20 were judged to be outstanding in a national contest sponsored by the National School Volunteer Program. Components of the programs were classified by frequency, producing a checklist of elements characteristic of an effective school volunteer program. Organization and management were found to be key factors in determining successful programs; senior citizens were the most likely candidates to fill gaps left by mothers who have entered the work force; volunteers who are specifically trained to work with the handicapped are becoming increasingly important; and students who are being served by volunteers have been all but ignored in evaluating those programs.

Holzmiller, Robert Joseph. Using Volunteer Aides in a K–5 Elementary School. Unpublished doctoral dissertation. University of Arizona. 1982.

The study found that teachers at an elementary school believed volunteers in clerical, supervisory, and noninitiated instructional tasks had very positive effects on their ability to teach students. Peer, student, and parent aides were helpful, but teachers most strongly supported community aides. In classrooms where volunteers were used, students exceeded anticipated achievement in reading and grammar as the result of teachers having more instructional time and as a result of activities by the volunteers themselves.

Jamer, T. Margaret. *School Volunteers.* New York: Public Education Association. 1961.

This is a general review of school volunteering. It includes chapters on organizing volunteer programs, administering them, selecting schools, preparing staff, recruiting and interviewing volunteers, and providing them with orientation. Another chapter profiles volunteers by age, educational background, and paid work experience. Another lists the different kinds of work volunteers can do and appraises volunteer programs in general. "Whatever the paths may be that the School Volunteer Program will follow," Jamer says, "it will continue to be true, as many teachers are now aware, that a volunteer can enrich the day for a child and that good must accrue whenever a good adult gives added attention to a child."

Janowitz, Gayle. *Helping Hands: Volunteer Work in Education.* Chicago: University of Chicago Press. 1965.

This is a seminal research book on the subject of school volunteers. Janowitz began working with volunteers in tutoring and homework help in 1962, at the Hyde Park Neighborhood Club Study Center in Chicago, applying the philosophy of respect for individual children that she had acquired from work with Bruno Bettelheim. In 1964, she started a 3-year demonstration and evaluation program with the support of the U.S. Office of Education, "to help improve our understanding of the problems of academic achievement and the role of the volunteer in education." The book was written while this research was still in progress.

Karnes, Merle B. The use of volunteers and parents in mainstreaming. *Viewpoints in Teaching and Learning* 55(3):44–56. 1979.

Feasible ways of mainstreaming the preschool child are viewed, and alternative ways of using volunteers and parents in this effort are delineated.

Katz, Douglas S. Planning to use volunteers. *Voc. Ed.* 58(3):28–29. April 1983.

Extensive planning by group process is important for establishing successful volunteer programs, as demonstrated by the process developed and tested in a number of demonstration programs nationwide.

Katz, Douglas S. *Volunteers and Voc Ed.* Information Series 271, National Center for Research in Vocational Education. Columbus: Ohio State University. 1984.

This report describes the benefits to vocational educators of involving volunteers in vocational programs and presents a model for planning and implementing a volunteer program. Guidelines are presented for monitoring program progress and evaluating the effects of the program. It includes a bibliography of related readings.

Lefkowitz, Leon J. Paraprofessionals: an administration/school board conspiracy? *Phi Delta Kappan* 54(8):546–547. 1973.

The failure of the teaching profession to react to the infiltration of paraprofessionals into the teaching ranks, a board conspiracy, suggests that teachers are doomed to second-class status.

Lewis, Mary Woolsey. *Volunteer Programs for Secondary Schools.* Palo Alto, Ca.: R&E Research Associates, Inc. 1978.

A handbook for teachers, administrators, volunteers, and especially volunteer coordinators, it describes the steps in program development; the responsibilities, resources, and rights of volunteers; and benefits to teachers and their concerns.

McClure, Milton Andrew. A Clinical Approach to Remedial Reading in the Secondary School Using Volunteer Community Aides: A Pilot Study. Unpublished doctoral dissertation. School of Education, Boston University. 1973.

The purpose of the study was to determine whether use of volunteer community aides in remedial reading classes at the high school level under direct supervision and guidance of a reading specialist would show a difference in reading attainment in contrast to classes where aides were not used. The study also attempted research on the proper use of teacher aides in the classroom. The period of time devoted to the study (9 weeks) was judged insufficient. It was hard to find volunteer aides, and reading classes lacked sufficient programmed materials. The researcher found no cognitive improvement, but attendance of students appeared to improve.

Merenda, Daniel W., Richard A. Lacey, and Virginia Robinson, eds. *A Practical Guide to Creating and Managing School/Community Partnerships.* Alexandria, Va.: National Association of Partners in Education. 1986.

The manual uses the 12-step process for program development, which sets forth a systematic approach to planning, implementing, and evaluating school volunteer programs. The manual is the curriculum for training academies in which teams from schools are trained to develop programs responsive to local needs and instructional objectives. It includes worksheets and self-assessments to be completed by participants for each chapter and an extensive appendix of sample materials.

Mosley, Elaine S. Christi. The Effects of a Classroom Volunteer Program on Achievement, Self-Concept, and Behavior Among Primary Grade Pupils. Unpublished doctoral dissertation. University of Oklahoma. 1982.

The researcher developed a volunteer program in four primary classrooms in each of four experimental schools; three classrooms from each of two schools served as controls. Tutoring was a major component of the volunteer program; volunteers were recruited and trained by the researcher. Findings did not show statistical evidence of positive effects of volunteers on achievement, self-concept, and school behavior, but the researcher remains convinced that trained volunteers working in classrooms are of vital importance to the quality of learning in public schools.

Mott Institute for Community Improvement. *The Use of School Volunteers.* East Lansing: Michigan State University. 1973.

The problems of using school volunteers are, according to this report from the Mott Institute, "more than offset by the results—a better community in which to educate children and adults." The bulk of the report covers the process of developing a program. There is a general discussion of problems encountered in program development, with suggestions for overcoming them, such as recruiting volunteers for a trial commitment of 8 weeks rather than the typical indefinite commitment and allowing prospective volunteers to participate in the development of their job descriptions.

Nathan, Joe. Wanted? School volunteers. *Teacher* 97(1):71–75. 1979.

Criticisms of school volunteer programs are discussed. The report suggests ways to counteract these concerns with a well-planned program. Appended is a directory listing three nationally validated volunteer programs and three other resource agencies.

Newman, Sally, Cindy Kramer, Charles Lyons, Rita O'Kane, and Eve Siegel. *Manual for Developing Intergenerational Programs in Schools.* Alexandria, Va.: National Association of Partners in Education. 1987.

The manual is intended to guide school systems through systematic procedures that will result in the creation of successful intergenerational programs. An intergenerational program is defined as "planned activities and experiences that are designed to bring the generations together for their mutual benefit." The authors are from the Generations Together project, Center for Social and Urban Research, University of Pittsburgh, Pennsylvania, and the San Francisco School Volunteer Program. An introduction discusses, "Why Intergenerational Programs in Schools?"

Plantec, Peter M., Joyce Hospodar, and Barbara Paramore. *Final Report on the Evaluation of Project Upswing's First Year.* Silver Spring, Md.: Operations Research, Inc. 1972.

This technical report describes the evaluation of the first year of Project

Upswing, a 2-year experimental study to determine the potential contribution of volunteers in helping young children overcome learning difficulties. Two groups of 1st grade children received tutoring from either trained or untrained volunteers; a third group received no tutoring. Volume I of the report profiles the participants. Volume II provides an analysis of tutoring results and final impressions of the project. An appendix gives facsimiles of evaluation questionnaires.

Powell, Bob. Volunteers in the schools: a positive approach to schooling. *National Association of Secondary School Principals Bulletin* 70(494):32–34. 1986.

The article describes the benefit of parent volunteer programs in schools, including maximizing teacher effectiveness and broadening parents' knowledge and appreciation of the educational process. It provides parent and teacher testimony and helpful hints for starting a successful volunteer program. The key is one principal's involvement.

Powers, Louis J. The Effectiveness of Volunteer College Student Helpers in Improving the Social and Academic Behaviors in Educable Mentally Retarded Children. Unpublished doctoral dissertation. University of Oregon. 1974.

The purpose of the study was to determine the effectiveness of college student helpers in modifying the academic and deviant social behaviors of mentally retarded children in special education classrooms. A secondary consideration was to determine if teachers trained in the use of behavior modification strategies would be more effective in bringing about such changes than teachers who were untrained in the use of those techniques. Powers found that reading achievement was significantly increased in all three groups after the college students assisted. Arithmetic achievement showed less improvement. Deviant social behavior also decreased when the students helped, although there was no more improvement when teachers were trained in behavior modification.

Rauner, Judy. People who need people—the volunteer component. *Momentum* 16(3):35–37. 1985.

The article explains steps in developing a volunteer program in a school. It also looks at trends in the number of volunteers, the competition for their services, volunteer expectations, and strength through networking.

Recruitment Leadership and Training Institute. *Volunteers in Education.* Philadelphia, Pa.: Recruitment Leadership and Training Institute. 1975.

This is a handbook for coordinators of volunteer programs, with chapters on funding sources and proposal preparation, organizing and developing a volunteer program, administering a program, recruiting volunteers, interviewing and assigning them, providing volunteer orientation and training as well as orientation and training of professional personnel, using students as volunteers, maintaining volunteer morale, and evaluating volunteer programs.

Reisner, Elizabeth R., Christene A. Petry, and Michele Armitage. *A Review of Programs Involving College Students as Tutors or Mentors in Grades K–12.* Washington, D.C.: Policy Studies Associates, Inc. 1989.

A survey and analysis were conducted of programs in colleges and universities in which college students served as volunteers in elementary and secondary schools. The study was mandated by the U.S. Congress in 1987 to determine whether college students can be effective tutors of children in Chapter I compensatory education programs.

Rick, Susan Snell. The Effects of a Volunteer Tutoring Program for First Graders with Learning Problems. Unpublished doctoral dissertation. St. Louis University. 1975.

The study attempted to determine if 1st graders with learning problems who are provided one-to-one volunteer tutorial assistance make greater gains in measures of reading, visual-motor integration, basic experiences, and intelligence than those not receiving one-to-one tutorial assistance. Rick concluded that there was greater mean improvement in reading by the tutored children than by those who were not tutored.

Ruffin, Santee C., Jr. School-business partnerships: why not? *Journal of Educational Public Relations* 7(2):4–9. 1984.

The article describes a volunteer program that used retired people to work in their neighborhood schools. Volunteers received training and provided an invaluable resource for students and teachers.

Sawyer, Diane J. Preparing volunteer tutors. *The Clearing House* 51(4):52–56. 1977.

The author points out that one-to-one tutoring is judged necessary for many disabled readers, but it is simply too costly to allocate the time of highly trained teachers to cover the magnitude of tutorial services that might be identified in any given school district. Volunteer or peer tutoring programs continue to be suggested as alternative means for providing one-to-one instruction in reading, but in practice tutoring programs are not generally successful over any long period of time. Sawyer believes this is because coordination of such programs tends to be informal and "added on" to the responsibilities of some interested teacher. She offers a brief orientation guide that teachers and administrators might use as the foundation for training sessions with inexperienced volunteers.

Schaffner, Deanne. A Study of the Effectiveness of Volunteers in the Classroom. Unpublished master's thesis. College of Education, University of Central Florida. 1987.

A survey was distributed to all instructional personnel in every elementary school (grades K–5) in Seminole County, Florida, asking if they had used volunteers, for how many hours a week, and the teachers' perceptions of the value of volunteers. Volunteers were perceived to make a difference in the classroom and to positively affect student learning and attitude.

Schulze, Sally Reddig. Evaluation of a Paraprofessional/Volunteer Program to Improve the Reading, Language, and Math Skills of Dyslexic Students. Unpublished doctoral dissertation. Department of Education, Case Western Reserve University. 1979.

Would a paraprofessional/volunteer program help solve the academic problems of dyslexic students by improving reading, language, and math skills? Schulze concluded that "paraprofessionals/volunteers can help dyslexic students achieve significant academic gains."

Seeley, David. Teachers' Choice: Whether to Accept the Bureaucratic Structure or Change to a New Partnership Model. Paper prepared for a symposium of the American Educational Research Association, Chicago, Illinois, 1985.

Seeley says most public school systems operate on the "delegation/ service delivery" model, in which teachers are the lowest-rung bureaucratic functionaries. He proposes a partnership model in which education is seen as a responsibility shared by many people who help a child learn. He discusses the advantages and drawbacks for teachers who share power with nonprofessionals.

Shannon, Thomas A. Build support through volunteers. *The American School Board Journal* 170(1):38,42. Alexandria, Va.

Shannon, executive director of the National School Boards Association (NSBA), cites a resolution adopted by NSBA's Delegate Assembly that reads: "NSBA urges local school districts to use volunteers as a means of enriching the learning experiences of students and to build school-community ties." He notes benefits to the instructional program, such as helping children to learn how to deal constructively with adults, and he describes volunteers as a "safety valve" for teachers. Reasons for hesitancy in using volunteers include lack of dependability and the "authority" issue—"the state turns its children over" to people who are qualified.

Slater, Marcia. Volunteers in the schools: a gift of service. *OSSC Bulletin* 23(2):1–37. 1979.

Increasing expenditures for education and a desire to more directly involve the public in the education of children have led many school districts to seek the assistance of school volunteers. This guidebook by the Oregon School Study Council (OSSC) discusses the growth of the volunteer movement, suggests procedures for establishing an organized school program, and appraises potential problems that might be encountered. An extensive appendix supplements the general text by offering specific suggestions for setting up, promoting, and recognizing volunteerism in the schools.

Steele, Sara. Extension-volunteer partnerships: cooperation with other agencies. *National Accountability Study and Evaluation of Extension and Volunteers.* Washington, D.C.: U.S. Department of Agriculture. 1988.

A 5-year (1983–1988) study was conducted by the Division of Continuing and Vocational Education, University of Wisconsin, Madison, and was sponsored by the Cooperative Extension System of the U.S. Department of Agriculture. One of five format papers on Extension-Volunteer Partnerships deals with cooperation with other agencies, including schools. Researchers conducted interviews with teachers, students, and volunteers in 12 counties in 12 states where extension volunteers worked in school projects involving curriculum, enrichment, and special cooperation. Descriptions are anecdotal; each includes a brief conclusion about the value of the project.

Streit, John Frederick. The Effect of an Instructional Volunteer Program on an Elementary School. Unpublished doctoral dissertation. Wayne State University. 1975.

The researcher surveyed volunteer effectiveness with children, training and placement of instructional volunteers, the volunteer-teacher relationship, and the impact of instructional volunteers on parents and the public. Survey results showed that students who were taught reading skills by volunteers made progress; there was positive change in attitude, social adjustment, overall academic achievement, and letter grades. The researcher found a discrepancy between what volunteers can do and what teachers will allow them to do and between what volunteers were trained to do and what they were asked to do by teachers. Teacher effectiveness was greater because of the instructional volunteer, but some teachers viewed instructional volunteers as a threat. Parents whose children worked with an instructional volunteer positively supported the program.

Sullivan, George, and Carol Florio. Senior citizens in education. *Social Policy* 7(3):103–106. 1976.

The authors describe a survey by the Academy for Education Developments, Inc., New York City, of 2,140 public school districts and 1,170 colleges and universities to determine how many people aged 65 and over were employed or contributing their services to education, what they were doing, and how well they were doing. Their report discusses volunteers, noting that traditionally the classroom has been the sacrosanct domain of the teacher and traces of this attitude linger.

Taltavull, Frances Adeline. An Investigation of the Effect of Volunteer Tutors and Readers on Reading Achievement of Fifth Grade Pupils in an Inner City School. Unpublished doctoral dissertation. Temple University. 1974.

A volunteer program was established in Philadelphia in 1963 as a pilot project cosponsored by the Citizens' Committee on Public Education and the School District. The researcher asked whether a tutoring program utilizing volunteer tutors can raise the reading achievement level of disadvantaged pupils. In the study, no control was exerted over the type of tutoring done; tutoring and reading sessions were limited to one 45-minute period per week for 8 weeks. Students made small gains, but they were not statistically significant and may have been due to the regular instructional program. The researcher recommended training for volunteers and two or three tutoring sessions per week for a full school year.

Tierce, Jerry Wood. The Role of the Secondary School Volunteer as Perceived by School Volunteer Coordinators. Unpublished doctoral dissertation. Texas A&M University. 1982.

A survey of coordinators of volunteer programs examined functions and tasks of secondary school volunteers and coordinators' perceptions of the difficulties, strengths, and domains for improvement of secondary volunteer programs.

Tierce, Jerry Wood, and Wayne C. Seelbach. Elders as school volunteers: an untapped resource. *Educational Gerontology* 13(1):33–41. 1987.

The article reviews the role and scope of school volunteerism and suggests ways to integrate Retired Senior Volunteer Program participants into school volunteer programs. The authors conclude that schools need the assistance of volunteers and that elders can benefit from serving in such socially meaningful roles.

Vassil, Thomas V., Oliver C. Harris, and Donald V. Fandetti. *The Perception of Public School Administrators Regarding Community Education Programs Sponsored by Maryland State Department of Education.* Baltimore, Md.: Maryland State Department of Education. 1988.

Data were collected by questionnaires completed by school principals and program coordinators on volunteer services to schools in Maryland. Volunteer services were found to be widely used throughout the school system in various ways such as assisting teachers, providing support for administrative and clerical services, and tutoring students. School programs have been impacted positively by volunteer services, including an increase in resources for instructional programs, improvement in students' behavior, and more use of school facilities after regular school hours. Volunteer services were perceived as making a significant contribution to school programs.

Walter, Franklin B. Volunteers . . . a vital resource for our schools. *School Slate* 485(June):2. 1988.

State Superintendent of Public Instruction Walter notes that Ohio's Minimum Standards for Elementary and Secondary Schools support involvement of volunteers in schools, and the Ohio Department of Education endorses the use of volunteers in schools. The article was published in the newsletter of the State of Ohio Board of Education.

Wyckoff, Lorna M. School volunteers face the issues. *Phi Delta Kappan* 58(10):755–756. 1977.

In this editorial director's report on a 1977 National School Volunteer Program conference, Wyckoff notes that the very success of volunteer projects has unsettled many professionals. The relationship between the educator and the volunteer remains unclear and is potentially volatile. The author wonders, for example, what would happen if teachers went on strike. A massive volunteer program might well undermine the walkout and force teachers back into the classroom with their demands unmet. Recent history already includes examples of principals and superintendents who have tried to keep school doors open with the help of volunteer aides. There is also fear that these days of budget constraints may lead to the permanent displacement of professionals by unpaid citizens.

Appendix C

Biographical Sketches of Committee Members and Staff

LEONARD BICKMAN (*Chair*) is professor of psychology and of public policy at Peabody College of Vanderbilt University and director of the Program Evaluation Laboratory. He is also senior research associate and director of the Mental Health Policy Center at the Vanderbilt Institute for Public Policy. He was most recently professor of psychology at Loyola University of Chicago and director of the Westinghouse Evaluation Institute. He is past president of the American Psychological Law Society and the Society for Psychological Studies of Social Issues. His undergraduate training was at the City College of New York, followed by a graduate degree and a doctorate in social psychology from Columbia University.

JOHN W. ALDEN is president, Alden Marketing Group, Inc. Formerly vice president for marketing, Falcon Microsystems, he has also held positions as manager, education marketing, Texas Instruments; vice president, Bank of America; senior policy analyst, U.S. Department of Health, Education, and Welfare; and director of institutional studies, University of Vermont. From 1976 to 1981 he served as executive director of the National School Volunteer Program. He has bachelor's and master's degrees from Bradley University and a doctorate from the University of Illinois.

STEPHEN R. DIAZ is associate professor, Teacher Education Program, California State University, San Bernardino, and staff research associate, University of California, San Diego. In addition to teaching, his professional experience includes work with the Multicultural Assessment Program (Title VII); the Institute for Personal Effectiveness in Children (San

Diego); the Rockefeller Counsel Project (San Diego); the Chicano Supportive Services at San Diego State University; the National Institute of Education; the Office of Civil Rights of the U.S. Department of Health, Education, and Welfare; and Upward Bound (San Diego). He is a member of the American Education Research Association, the Association of Mexican-American Educators, the Council on Anthropology and Education, and the National Association for Bilingual Education. He has a bachelor's degree from the University of San Diego, a master's degree in education from San Diego State University, and a doctorate in education from Harvard University.

PAUL L. EVANS is education industry consultant, IBM Educational Systems. His primary area of interest is applying advanced and emerging multimedia technologies to enhance knowledge representation, learning, and understanding. Previously, he was program manager for policy studies in science and mathematics education at the National Science Foundation where he was editor of *The Science Education Databook;* he has also been a university professor. In the late 1960s, he was a member of the National Teacher Corps, teaching in remote mountain schools in Southern Appalachia. He is a member of the American Psychological Association, the American Association for the Advancement of Science, the American Educational Research Association, and the World Future Society. He holds a bachelor's degree from the University of South Carolina, a graduate degree from the College of William and Mary, and a doctorate in educational psychology from the University of Georgia.

MARVIN LAZERSON is dean and George and Diane Weiss Professor at the Graduate School of Education, University of Pennsylvania. He is author and coauthor of numerous books and articles on educational history and educational policy and has taught at the Harvard Graduate School of Education, the University of British Columbia, Stanford University, and the University of Washington. His research interests include the history of equality and excellence in education, the origins of public policy, the history of early childhood education, and the relationship between work and schooling. Both his bachelor's and master's degrees are from Columbia University; his doctorate in history is from Harvard University.

DANIEL B. LEVINE served as consultant to the committee. As a senior associate with the Committee on National Statistics of the National Research Council, he has served as the director for several studies, including an evaluation of the National Center for Education Statistics, a review of the system of immigration statistics, and a workshop on income and poverty statistics. Formerly with the Bureau of the Census, he was deputy director and also served as acting director. His interests are in the management of statistical systems and in the collection, processing, and presentation of statistical information, particularly through the conduct of large-scale surveys and censuses. He is a fellow of the American Statistical Association and a member of the International Statistical Institute. He received a bachelor's degree from George Washington University and a master's degree in economics from Columbia University.

FLORETTA DUKE MCKENZIE is president of the McKenzie Group, a comprehensive educational consulting firm, and a distinguished visiting professor, Graduate School of Education, Harvard University. Formerly, she was superintendent and chief state school officer for the Washington, D.C., public schools, the 21st largest school system in the nation. She has also served as deputy assistant secretary, Office of School Improvement, U.S. Department of Education; U.S. delegate to UNESCO; deputy superintendent of schools, Montgomery County (Md.) public schools; and assistant deputy superintendent, Maryland State Department of Education. She serves on the boards of the National Geographic Society, Potomac Electric Power Company, Riggs National Corporation, George Washington University, WETA public television, Reading Is Fundamental, and the Boy Scouts of America. Her undergraduate work was at D.C. Teacher's College, followed by a graduate degree from Howard University and a doctorate in education from George Washington University.

DANIEL W. MERENDA is executive director of the National Association of Partners in Education. Previously, he served as executive director of the National School Volunteer Program, coming to that position with a background in volunteer activities and with experience as a teacher, school superintendent, and federal administrator. His bachelor's degree is from Western Michigan University and his master's degree in English is from the State University of New York.

BERNARD MICHAEL was study director for the Committee on the Use of School Volunteers and was formerly executive director of the Federal Interagency Committee on Education of the U.S. Department of Health, Education, and Welfare. He also served as director of evaluation on vocational education and manpower training in the Office of Education and as senior manpower economist and statistician with the Bureau of Labor Statistics. He also was executive vice president of Information Dynamics, Inc. He received a bachelor's degree from George Washington University and a master's degree in economics from Columbia University.

CAROL L. MOCK is assistant professor, Department of Political Science and Institute of Government and Public Affairs, University of California at Berkeley, where she received her doctorate. In addition to having been a visiting assistant professor in higher education at the University of California at Los Angeles, she has been the recipient of several academic achievement awards and fellowships, including a Danforth fellowship. She has served on several university and public service committees in the University of California system and was the first student regent of the University of California. Her current research interests focus on the development of a theory of organizational design based on the formal logic of cybernetics and information theory and on the relationship between public policy and modernization and other changes in the 50 states.

PENELOPE L. PETERSON is professor of educational psychology and teacher education at Michigan State University and codirector of the Institute for Research on Teaching and the Center for Learning and Teaching of Elementary Subjects. She is also a senior researcher at the Center for Policy Research in Education funded by the U.S. Department of Education. Previously, she was Sears-Bascom Professor of Educational Psychology at the University of Wisconsin, Madison. She is coeditor of *Research on Teaching: Concepts, Findings and Implications,* and *The Social Context of Instruction: Group Organization and Group Processes.* In 1980 she received the Palmer O. Johnson Award from the American Educational Research Association (AERA) for her article on teachers' decision making during interactive classroom teaching. In 1986 she received the Raymond B. Cattell Early Career Award for her outstanding programmatic research on effective teaching and student mediation of instruction. She is the editor of the AERA's *Review of Educational Research,* AERA vice president for Division C (Learning and Instruction), and a consultant to the National Board for Professional Teaching Standards. She holds both a master's degree and a doctorate in educational psychology from Stanford University.

VIRGINIA ROBINSON served as consultant to the committee. A journalist who has written extensively on the subject of school volunteerism, she is a former editor of *Education Times* and *Education Daily* and currently edits *Partners in Education* for the National Association of Partners in Education. She was a research associate in education at George Washington University in Washington, D.C., and is the author of a number of reports on education and school volunteerism.

JOYCE W. ROGERS is secretary-treasurer of the board of directors of the National School Boards Association. She has also served on the Portland, Maine, Superintending School Committee since 1974. She is past president of the Maine School Boards Association and was a planner on the Greater Portland Planning Commission. Previously, she worked as an advertising executive at Little, Brown; as a columnist for the Portland *Press Herald;* and as a consultant to the U.S. Department of Education, the executive board of the National Council for Accreditation of Teacher Education, and the board of directors of the National Organization for Student Assistance Programs. She has been a member of the Maine Advisory Council on Vocational Education; the Maine Certification Appeals Board; and the Maine Advisory Councils for Accreditation Standards, Graduation Standards, School Administrative Units, and Teacher Certification. Rogers also served as a member of the Rockefeller Arts Award Advisory Panel. She has a bachelor's degree from Mt. St. Mary College and a graduate degree from Oxford University.

GILBERT T. SEWALL is codirector of the Educational Excellence Network, a confederation of educators, scholars, and journalists headquartered at Teachers College, Columbia University. He is the author of the award-winning book, *Necessary Lessons: Decline and Renewal in American Schools,* and coauthor of *After Hiroshima: America Since 1945.* He has written for many publications, including *Newsweek, Fortune, The Wall Street Journal,* and *The New York Times.* He has contributed to many academic and educational journals and wrote the recent nationally acclaimed report, *American History Textbooks: An Assessment of Quality.* Previously, he taught American history and developed honors courses in economics and in the history of art at the Phillips Academy. He has been a consultant to the Rockefeller and Exxon education foundations and to the U.S. Department of Education. Sewall received a bachelor's degree from the University of California at Berkeley, a master's degree from Brown University, and a master's degree in journalism from Columbia University.

MANYA S. UNGAR has been a volunteer most of her adult life. In 1987, she was elected to a 2-year term as president of the national Parent-Teachers Association (PTA), which is the fifth largest association in the United States. She has also been active in the international/intercultural student exchange program of the American Field Service and in the League of Women Voters in Scotch Plains, New Jersey. Currently, she serves on the boards of the New Jersey Public Education Institute, the Mathematical Sciences Education Board, the Council for the Advancement of Citizenship, and Civitas. She is a member of Independent Sector's Communications and Education Subcommittee. She was recently appointed to the

Arts Education Advisory Committee for the National Endowment for the Arts and the National Commission for Drug Free Schools. She recently completed her tenure as cochair of the Education Committee for the Martin Luther King, Jr., Federal Holiday Commission and service on the White House Conference for a Drug-Free America as well as the Advisory Committee for the Education Commission of the States.

CAROL H. WEISS is a professor at the Harvard Graduate School of Education and has been a visiting professor at Arizona State University. She also has been associated with the Center for the Social Sciences and the Bureau of Applied Social Research at Columbia University. She is the author of seven books and 80 articles, most recently *Reporting of Social Science in the National Media* (1988) with E. Singer, and has written extensively on program evaluation, including the books *Evaluation Research* and *Evaluating Action Programs*. Her recent activities have included serving as guest scholar at the Brookings Institution; senior fellow in the Office of Research, U.S. Department of Education; and visiting scholar at the General Accounting Office. Her undergraduate training was at Cornell University, followed by a master's degree and a doctorate in psychology from Columbia University.

BARBARA J. YENTZER is special assistant for education and outreach, National Education Association, and chair of the Coalition for Parental Involvement in Education. She serves as a member of the board of directors of the Council for the Advancement of Citizenship, the board of directors of the Alliance for Environmental Education, and the Education Advisory Committee for the National Commission on the Bicentennial of the U.S. Constitution. She served as assistant regional director of the western region for the National Education Association from 1978 to 1984. She has held positions as negotiations specialist, National Education Association; UniServ/field representative, Pennsylvania State Education Association; and as teacher, instructor, and curriculum coordinator in the Pennsylvania school districts of Council Rock and Palisades and in Elgin, Oklahoma. She received a bachelor's degree from Temple University, a master's degree from Trenton State College, and has done postgraduate work at Temple University, Newark State College, the University of California at Irvine, and San Jose State College.